# Stern's Guide To
# Disney
# Collectibles

## Second Series

# Stern's Guide To
# Disney
# Collectibles

## Second Series

## Michael Stern

**COLLECTOR BOOKS**

*A Division of Schroeder Publishing Co., Inc.*

## *Searching For A Publisher?*

We are always looking for knowledgeable people considered to be experts in their fields. If you feel that there is a real need for a book on your collectible subject and have a large comprehensive collection, contact Collector Books.

Additional copies of this book may be ordered from:

Collector Books
P.O. Box 3009
Paducah, KY  42002-3009

@ $14.95 Add $2.00 for postage and handling.

Copyright:  Michael Stern, 1991
Values Updated, 1995

This book or any part  thereof may not be reproduced without the written consent of the Author and Publisher.

Printed by IMAGE GRAPHICS, INC., Paducah, Kentucky

# Dedication

This book is dedicated to my wife, Merrill, and my daughters, Jenny and Lisa, for all their support and encouragement.

# Acknowledgments

To all the good friends, all over the country, I have made in my Disneyana dealings.

To all the collectors whose persistent search for Disneyana is rewarded when they find that rare piece they've been hoping one day will appear.

To Chuck Young for his incredible photography.

# Contents

# Introduction

There's still no greater thrill than to find a Disneyana collectible not previously seen before. Since the last edition was published, the Disneyana marketplace has gone through quite a transformation. The most basic economic principle of supply and demand has encompassed the collecting of Disney memorabilia. The demand for these artifacts of the past has grown dramatically and the supply has just as dramatically decreased. This is not to say that one cannot find Disneyana available; it's just that it's most difficult because the number of collectors has grown.

Lack of supply, and more demand for it, has pushed the prices of high-quality, early Disneyana memorabilia much higher. Who could have fathomed that a black and white cell from "Orphan's Benefit" would have sold for $450,000.00 or that a Mickey Mouse Cowboy Knickerbocker Doll would fetch $16,000.00 at auction.

Disneyana is a comic art form and the appreciation of prices of this art form, parallels the increase in the values of all forms of artwork. It could be said that the owning of Disneyana is like owning quality stocks and bonds -- an excellent investment that increases in value on a yearly basis.

The added value is that whereas stock and bonds are tucked away in a safe or vault; your Disneyana collectibles can be displayed and enjoyed on a daily basis. I call it "double appreciation."

Mickey Mouse and the gang continue to be the most sought after of any characters in the comic collectible field. With the addition of Disney theme parks in Europe and Japan, Disneyana collecting has become international. Each day more and more people join the fold of Mickey Mouse fanatics who live and breathe for that new piece to add to their collection.

The field of Disneyana collectors is growing and the intensity of these Disney enthusiasts is overwhelming. Many publications and auction catalogs are available for those wishing to acquire Disney memorabilia through the mail. The following are publications that contain valuable information on a variety of Disneyana topics.

## Collectors Showcase
P.O. Box 837
Tulsa, OK 74101

## Antique Toy World
P.O. Box 34509
Chicago, IL 60634

## Storyboard Magazine
2512 Artesia Boulevard
Redondo Beach, CA 90278-9984

The following are reputable mail and phone bid auction houses that contain Disneyana.

## Hake's Americana & Collectibles
P.O. Box 1444
York, PA 17405
(717) 848-1333

## Smith House Toy Sales
P.O. Box 336
Eliot, ME 03903
(207) 439-4614

## New England Auction Gallery
P.O. Box 2273
W. Peabody, MA 01960-7273
(503) 535-3140

All of the photographs in this book are taken from my personal collection. I have been collecting for six years. It took a lot of leg work, a multitude of patience, and a lot of luck being in the right place at the right time. All of these items have been acquired since the publication of the first book. Disney collectibles are still out there. They do exist and, though it's not always easy, they can be found by today's collectors.

My hope is that this book will help assist and broaden one's scope so that when acquiring a piece of Disney memorabilia, it can be dated and its price put into perspective.

# Pie-eyed Mickey and Minnie Mouse

Mickey Mouse was created in 1928, and since his inception, has been the backbone of the Disney dynasty. Since Steamboat Willie, his first cartoon, was released on November 18, 1928, Mickey Mouse became an immediate and unqualified success. Mickey Mouse may be the most recognized and perfect graphic symbol of any cartoon character ever created. He is the most sought after in the nostalgia marketplace and is the superstar of all Disneyana collectibles. Mickey and Minnie Mouse memorabilia became pop culture artifacts.

This chapter is titled "Pie-eyed Mickey and Minnie," and all items pictured are from the years 1928-1938. This is the period from which sophisticated Mickey Mouse "memorabiliacs" feel produced the finest and most valuable collector's items. Many sophisticated collectors seek only items manufac-

tured from these "golden" years. Mickey Mouse and Minnie Mouse from this period were created as primitive and impish rodents and are most recognizable by their pie-shaped eyes. The eyes look as though a sliver of pie has been removed from them leaving a blank indention.

Mickey and Minnie Mouse of the 1930's have the look of pot-bellied rodents; a thin, long, mouse-like tail; stove pipe arms and legs; overly large, bulbous shoes; two button shorts; thick, four-finger, glove-like hands and black balloon ears.

Walt Disney described his early Mouse: "His head is a circle with an oblong circle for a snout. The ears are also circles so they can be drawn the same, no matter how he turns his head. His body is like a pear with a long tail."

Early Mickey and Minnie Mouse are in direct

contrast to their latter day counter-parts who are pink faced, more humanoid, and minus the tail. The pie eyes were filled with black circles. Through the years, Mickey Mouse also shed his pot belly.

The various items of the 1930's are distinguishable by their markings. Usually, these items are marked "Walt E. Disney," "Walt Disney," or "Walt Disney Enterprises." On occasion, just the initials "W.D.E." were utilized. Some items were manufactured with stick-on labels or import stamps that through the years have fallen off or been removed.

Pie-eyed Mickey was featured in every imaginable type of toy and household item. Items that carried his image became overnight best sellers. Mickey and Minnie Mouse were constant house guests, and it was rare indeed to go through a normal day without being influenced by Disney's Mouse.

The pictorial section on pie-eyed Mickey opens with an extremely rare toy. Celluloid items have become the hardest to find and thus are the most desired by advanced collectors. **Plate 1, Mickey Mouse on Pluto** is a great example of a celluloid action toy. It utilizes a very simple early wind-up mechanism that simulates the rocking motion. Celluloid is hard to find in good condition, because though it was relatively durable, it was lightweight and extremely delicate and since they were children's toys, they often got crushed. Celluloid was also highly flammable. This piece is enhanced because both characters are made of celluloid.

Another unusual celluloid toy is **Mickey Mouse Hobby Horse** pictured in **Plate 2.** Many times a toy manufacturer would enhance the value of his toy by adding Mickey Mouse to it. The celluloid allowed Mickey Mouse to be reproduced in explicit detail and in vibrant color. The hobby horse is made of wood and is hand painted. The use of a simple spring mechanism is employed in this toy.

Early Mickey Mouse dolls are rapidly growing in popularity. They are excellent representations of the early pie-eyed Mickey Mouse. Dean's Rag Book Company of England produced some of the earliest dolls. In **Plates 3 and 4, two of the eight different sizes of Dean's Rag Doll Mickey Mouse** are pictured. The dolls are made of velvet with flat felt ears and hands. They are known for their thinner bodies, five-fingered hands and, most notable, their toothy sneer. Walt Disney was very unhappy with the Dean's Rag look because it petrified children. He banned further export of this doll. The tag on the five-inch doll reads, "Al Toys are Hygienic, Mickey Mouse, Made in England by Dean's Rag Book

Company, Ltd."

A more appealing **Cowboy Mickey Mouse Doll** is in **Plate 5**. This doll was manufactured by the Knickerbocker Toy Company and is the largest size of this doll standing two feet tall. Mickey Mouse dolls dressed in various costumes command a much higher price and are in more demand. This Cowboy Mickey Mouse is complete with original hat, kerchief, chaps and holster; two small metal guns are missing. Recently, the smaller version sold for $16,000.00 at an auction exceeding all previous records for a Mickey Mouse doll.

Another company that manufactured early dolls was the Margarete Steiff Company. **In Plates 6, 7 and 8, three different sizes of the Steiff dolls** are represented. The Steiff trademark is a metal tag punched through the left ear with a paper tag attached to it. The small five-inch Steiff is made of felt while all other sizes were made of velvet. All buttons on the dolls are mother-of-pearl. All Steiffs had a paper label on the front of the doll as shown in Plate 6. This label can increase the price of the doll by over $1,000.00.

Many Mickey Mouse toys gained overnight success and had a major impact on the companies that manufactured them. One such company is the Ingersoll-Waterbury Company. In 1933, they were on the verge of bankruptcy when a deal was struck to produce all types of Mickey Mouse watches. In **Plate 9, an Ingersoll English Mickey Mouse Pocket Watch** is pictured. The best description of this rare watch is from Robert Lesser's book, "A Celebration of Comic Art and Memorabilia." He details this pocket watch as: "One of the most beautiful pictures of Mickey Mouse ever put on the face of a watch or on anything. Here Mickey has a five o' clock shadow, a big grin, a long tail and is dressed to the nines in upper class English fashion and sporty orange gloves. The watch faces are made from a high gloss paper, and the rotating second hand has three Mickey Mouses chasing one another. These English Mickeys are extremely rare and very high priced when found. None have been found in the colorful Mickey Mouse decorated boxes."

The greatest find for a serious bisque collector is finding a boxed set. Most people discarded the boxes when they set their figurines out for display. The boxed set in **Plate 10** is the **Two Pals Set**. Mickey and Minnie Mouse are four inches tall. The original sticker is on the bottom of Mickey Mouse's foot. It is marked, "Mickey Mouse copy 1920, 1930 by Walter Disney." The boxed set in **Plate 11** is the **Three**

**Musicians Bisque.** They are each 3½ inches tall.

The **Mickey Mouse Lunch Kit** in **Plate 12** is one of the best examples of early tin lithography. It is the rarest and most expensive of any lunch box ever produced of any character. The lunch kit comes with its original lunch tray that is removable. The condition of this piece -- no wear or rust -- enhances its value tremendously. The lunch kit was made by the Gueder Paeschke and Frey Company and is so hard to locate that high prices have been paid for these in only fair condition.

The **Mickey Mouse Circus Train** pictured in **Plate 13** was made by the Lionel Train Company. It is one of the top five sought after pieces in Disney-ana collecting. Mickey Mouse stokes the engine with a continuous up-and-down movement which gives the illusion of shoveling coal. The engine weighs over one pound and the lithography on the three dining cars is phenomenal. Included with the train is a beautiful paper tent, a five-inch composition figure used as a circus barker, a miniature paper gas station, cardboard cutouts of Mickey and Minnie Mouse and twelve admission tickets. A complete set with box can command a price of over $10,000.00.

The **Mickey Mouse Advertising Sign** showcased in **Plate 14** is very unusual and the story behind it makes it even more incredible. This sign was made for a 50-gallon oil drum and put on the drums containing RPM oil. Walt Disney, feeling that the image of Mickey Mouse was not best suited for oil drums, cancelled the contract after a short period of time. I know of no other collector having this piece. It's easy to believe because how many people would think oil drum lids would one day become a Disneyana collectible.

The **Mickey Mouse Lamp** pictured in **Plate 15** was made by the Soreng-Manegold Company and is shown with its original paper parchment shade. The base is made of tin. The **lamp, with its original Mickey Mouse Filament**, is shown in **Plate 16**. When lit, a "neon" effect is generated by the filament and lights up the entire room.

The early merchandising effort left no stone unturned. An excellent gift idea was the **Mickey Mouse Silver-Plated Porringer** pictured in **Plate 17**. This was produced by the International Silver Company and featured Horace Horsecollar, one of the earliest Disney characters. The porringer is shown with its original box and price tag. The selling price of $2.50 made this an expensive gift in the 1930's.

To wake up the morning with Mickey Mouse, two different alarm clocks were utilized. In **Plate 18** is the **Electric Mickey Mouse Alarm Clock** and in **Plate 19** the **Wind-Up Wagging Head Alarm Clock** is pictured. Both were made by Ingersoll. The electric clock is 4¼" square and has a Waterbury Company paper band around the top and sides highlighting all the early Disney characters. The second hand is controlled by a metal revolving Mickey Mouse. The wagging head alarm clock had to be wound daily.

An extremely rare bisque is pictured in **Plate 20**. This particular **Mickey Mouse in a Bisque Canoe** is a size that has never previously been documented. The canoe is five inches long. It is rare to find any bisque that incorporates the use of Mickey Mouse and an object; in this case a canoe. This bisque would be a welcome addition to even the most sophisticated collector's display shelf.

The Mickey Mouse in **Plate 21** is referred to as a **"Rat-Faced" Mickey Mouse.** It was made in Germany and is pressed wood. The label on the foot reads, "Mickey Maus, Walt. E. Disney." Many collectors seek and prefer this "rat-faced" look.

**Balancing Mickey Mouse** is pictured in **Plate 22**. This painted wooden Mickey Mouse can be manipulated into a variety of stances. It is the only wooden toy that can stand on a foot or a hand because of its unique "suction cup" hands. It is 4½" inches tall and was distributed by the George Borgfeldt Company. The ears are also made of wood and his face displays the characteristics of a very early Mickey Mouse. The label crossing his stomach is also unique in its appearance and the way it is lettered.

Pictured in **Plate 23 and 24** is the Mystery Piece of Disneyana. I cannot locate anyone who has ever seen or heard of this piece. It is not handmade but a production piece. The tunnel is made of papier-mache and is one foot in length. The opening is eleven inches high. Please let me know if you can identify this Disney mystery tunnel.

The **Mickey Mouse Piano** pictured in **Plate 25** is one of the most desirable pieces of early Disneyana. The piano is ten inches long and was manufactured by the Marks Bros. Company in 1935 and sold for $1.00. It is a combination of wood, glass and cardboard. As each key is punched, a cardboard Mickey and Minnie Mouse perform an animated dance. The background is lithographed paper glued to the back of the piano itself.

*Plate 1* - **MICKEY MOUSE ON PLUTO** is an unusual celluloid wind-up with a wooden base. It features a very simple early wind-up mechanism that simulates the rocking motion.

*Plate 2* - **HOBBY HORSE MICKEY MOUSE** is made of celluloid and uses a spring mechanism. Celluloid is a light-weight and extremely delicate plastic; making it difficult to find a figurine in excellent condition.

*Plate 3* - **DEAN'S RAG DOLL MICKEY MOUSE** is five inches tall. These dolls are noted for their thinner bodies, five-fingered hands and their toothy sneer. The tag reads "Al Toys are Hygienic, Mickey Mouse, Made in England by Dean's Rag Book Co., Ltd."

*Plate 4* - **DEAN'S RAG DOLL MICKEY MOUSE** is eight inches tall. Walt Disney was very unhappy with this doll's rat-look because it frightened children. Disney banned further export of this doll from England.

*Plate 5* - **COWBOY MICKEY MOUSE DOLL** is two feet tall and was manufactured by the Knickerbocker Toy Company. Mickey Mouse dolls dressed in various costumes command a much higher price and are in more demand. The Cowboy Mickey Mouse is complete with original hat, kerchief, chaps and holster.

*Plate 6* - **MICKEY MOUSE STEIFF DOLL** was produced by the Margarete Steiff Company of Germany. The doll is seven inches tall and has the original tag sewn into his stomach.

*Plate 7* - **MICKEY MOUSE STEIFF DOLL** is nine inches tall and made of velvet. The Steiff trademark is a metal tag punched through the left ear.

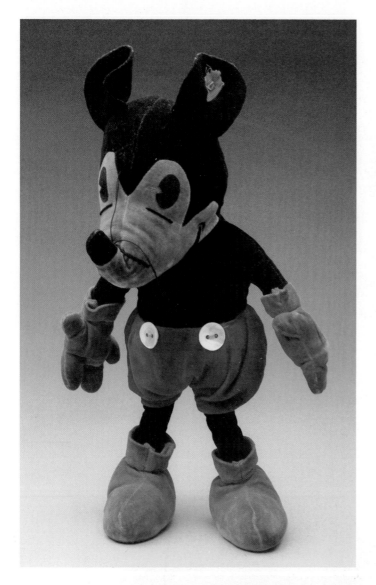

*Plate 8* - **MICKEY MOUSE STEIFF DOLL** is 11 inches tall. The doll has both the metal tag and paper tag punched through the left ear. All buttons on Steiff dolls are mother-of-pearl.

*Plate 9* - **MICKEY MOUSE ENGLISH POCKET WATCH** was made by the Ingersoll-Waterbury Company. It features a pink-faced Mickey wearing five-fingered gloves. The watch is marked, "Foreign." The English box, which is also marked "Foreign" inside, is one of the few known to exist.

*Plate 10* - **THE TWO PALS BOXED BISQUE SET** was made in Japan. Mickey and Minnie are four inches tall. The original sticker on the bottom of Mickey Mouse's foot is marked, "Mickey Mouse copy 1928, 1930 by Walter Disney."

*Plate 11* - **MUSICIAN BOXED BISQUE SET** was manufactured in Japan. The figures are hand painted and are 3½ inches tall. The colorful box dramatically increases the value of this piece.

*Plate 12* - **MICKEY MOUSE LUNCH KIT** was made by the Gueder, Paeschke and Frey Company. It is a fine example of early tin lithography. The lunch kit comes with a lunch tray that is removable and is the most rare and most expensive lunch box ever produced of any character.

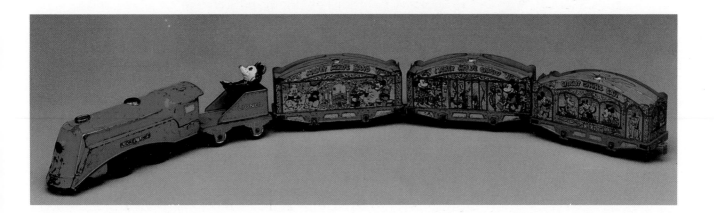

*Plate 13* - **MICKEY MOUSE CIRCUS TRAIN** was made by the Lionel Train Company. Included with the train was a beautiful paper tent, a five-inch composition Mickey Mouse circus barker, a miniature paper gas station, paper tent, cardboard Mickey and Minnie Mouse and twelve admission tickets.

*Plate 14 -* **MICKEY MOUSE OIL DRUM LID** was made for a 50-gallon oil drum manufactured for RPM oil. Walt Disney felt that Mickey Mouse was not best suited for oil drums and cancelled the contract after a short period of time.

*Plate 15 -* **MICKEY MOUSE ELECTRIC LAMP** was produced by the Soreng-Manegold Company. The lamp shade was made of parchment paper and the base is metal.

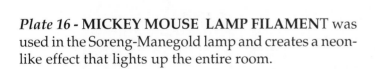

*Plate 16 -* **MICKEY MOUSE LAMP FILAMEN**T was used in the Soreng-Manegold lamp and creates a neon-like effect that lights up the entire room.

*Plate 17* - **MICKEY MOUSE PORRINGER** was manufactured by the International Silver Company. The porringer is shown with its original box and price tag. In the 1930's it sold for $2.50, making it an expensive gift.

*Plate 18* - **MICKEY MOUSE ELECTRIC ALARM CLOCK** was made by Ingersoll-Waterbury Company. It is 4¼" square and has a paper band stretching around the top and sides highlighting all the early Disney characters. The second hand is controlled by a metal revolving Mickey Mouse.

*Plate 19* - **MICKEY MOUSE WIND-UP ALARM CLOCK** was made by the Ingersoll-Waterbury Company. It is referred to as the wagging head alarm clock and had to be wound daily.

*Plate 20* - **MICKEY MOUSE IN CA-NOE BISQUE** was made in Japan. The canoe is five inches long which is oversized compared to others known to exist. It is rare to find any bisque that incorporates Mickey Mouse and an object; in this case a canoe.

*Plate 21* - **RAT-FACED GERMAN MICKEY MOUSE** is made of pressed wood. Mickey Mouse has the very early "rat-faced" look with a toothy grin. The label on the foot reads "Mickey Maus, Walt. E. Disney." A good example of a German Mickey Maus.

*Plate 22* - **BALANCING MICKEY MOUSE** is the only painted wooden Mickey Mouse that can be positioned into a variety of stances. Because of his unique suction cup hands he can stand on one foot or one hand. Mickey Mouse is 4½" tall.

*Plate 23* - **MICKEY MOUSE MYSTERY TUNNEL** is a manufactured product made of papier-mache and is one foot long by eleven inches high. No one has been able to identify the maker and its usage.

*Plate 24* - **MICKEY MOUSE MYSTERY TUNNEL** is a real mystery.

*Plate 25 - MICKEY & MINNIE MOUSE PIANO* was made by the Marks Brothers Company and is ten inches wide. As each key is pushed down, a cardboard Mickey and Minnie Mouse perform an animated dance.

*Plate 26 - MICKEY MOUSE WHIRLYGIG* was manufactured in Japan and distributed by the George Borgfeldt Company. This early tin wind-up moves in a circular pattern when wound. The celluloid umbrella and balls also revolve as the cart moves. Mickey Mouse is made of celluloid.

*Plate 27* - **MICKEY MOUSE BAGATELLE** was made by the Marks Brothers Company. This game is made of wood and is played with marbles. The bagatelle is one of the largest early Disney pieces measuring two feet tall and one foot wide.

*Plate 28* - **MICKEY MOUSE MOVIE JECTOR** was made by the Movie Jector Company. It was one of the first projectors used to show Mickey Mouse cartoons. The original film "Winning the Derby" is included with the movie jector.

*Plate 29* - **MICKEY MOUSE PENCIL BOX AND STORE ADVERTISEMENTS** were made by the Dixon USA Company and are marked, "Walt Disney Enterprises". The original store advertisement states, "Have you seen the Mickey Mouse Pencil Boxes at the Big School Sale?"

*Plate 30* - **MICKEY MOUSE WASHING MACHINE** is made of tin and was produced by the Ohio Art Company. It is an excellent piece of early tin lithography.

*Plate 31 -* **MICKEY MOUSE TARGET GAME** was made by the Marks Brothers Company. Shown with the target are the enameled steel spring loaded gun and six rubber-tipped vacuum cup darts. This is the largest version made.

*Plate 32 -* **MICKEY MOUSE TOY SLIDES** were made by Ensign Limited, London, and the glass slides were produced with permission of Walter E. Disney. It is interesting to note that the pictures on the box are courtesy of Dean & Son, manufacturers of early dolls.

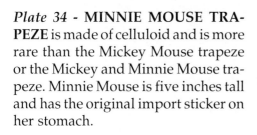

*Plate 33* - **MINNIE MOUSE SILVER CUP** was made by the International Silver Company. This was a popular child's gift in the 1930's.

*Plate 34* - **MINNIE MOUSE TRAPEZE** is made of celluloid and is more rare than the Mickey Mouse trapeze or the Mickey and Minnie Mouse trapeze. Minnie Mouse is five inches tall and has the original import sticker on her stomach.

*Plate 35 -* **MICKEY MOUSE CANE** is 34 inches long and features the Fun-E-Flex Mickey Mouse as the cane handle.

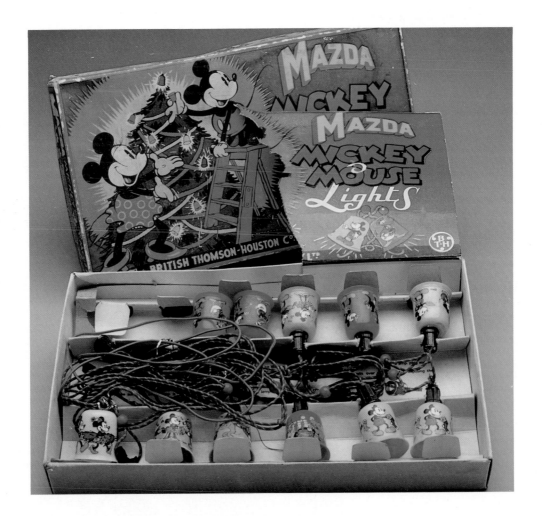

*Plate 36 -* **MICKEY MOUSE LIGHTS** were produced by the Thomson-Houston Company of England. These are the English versions of the American Noma Christmas lights. The lights are housed in shades decorated with early Disney characters.

*Plate 37 -* **MICKEY MOUSE FIGURAL PENCIL BOX** was a Dixon USA product. Included with the pencil box is the original Mickey Mouse pencil and ruler. This is the only paper figural pencil box produced by Dixon.

*Plate 38 -* **MICKEY MOUSE TEA SET** was made by the Ohio Art Company and is all tin. Included in the set are 13 tin lithographed pieces including creamer and teapot. The box does not have Disney graphics which is common.

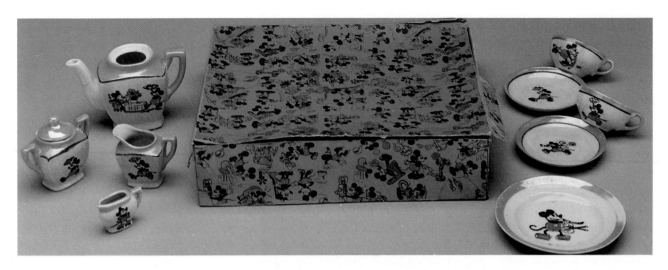

*Plate 39 -* **MICKEY MOUSE CHINA TEA SET** was made in Japan and features different scenes of Mickey and Minnie Mouse on each piece. The border colors are similar. Only the pitcher, creamer and sugar container are marked, "Walt Disney Enterprises."

*Plate 40 -* **MICKEY MOUSE TAMBORINE and GUITAR** were manufactured by the Noble Cooley Company. These are rare musical instruments and are sought for their vivid, colorful graphics. They are marked, "Walt Disney Enterprises."

*Plate 41 -* **MICKEY MOUSE BELLS** were made by Noma Light Company and were used on Christmas trees. Each bell is marked, "W.D."

*Plate 42 -* MICKEY AND MINNIE MOUSE PATTERNS FOR DOLLS were sold in the 1930's and came in all shapes and sizes. The dolls can be dated by their fingers and the characteristics of their shoes.

*Plate 43* - **MICKEY MOUSE AND MINNIE MOUSE PATTERN DOLLS** were hand-made in the 1930's by using various patterns available at the local stores. Many patterns were made by the McCall Company.

*Plate 44* - **Item A - MICKEY MOUSE PRINTING BLOCKS** were used with a stamp pad or printing press to create the Mickey Mouse image.

**Item B - CELLULOID MICKEY MOUSE ON WOODEN BRIDGE** was made in Japan and came with many different combinations and colors of Mickey Mouse.

*Plate 45* - **MINNIE MOUSE PIN CUSHION** is a rare bisque piece. It is unusual to find a bisque figurine that features an inanimate object with Mickey or Minnie Mouse.

*Plate 46* - **MICKEY MOUSE KNICKERBOCKER DOLL** is 21" tall with composition shoes and is the largest Knickerbocker doll produced. This doll has the original tag tied to his hand. It is a beautiful representation of early Mickey Mouse.

*Plate 47 -* **Item A - MICKEY MOUSE PENCIL SHARPENER** is made of celluloid and is 2½ inches tall. The metal sharpener is encased in Mickey Mouse's body.

**Item B - MICKEY MOUSE NURSERY DOLL** is made of celluloid and stands five inches tall. Both arms and legs are movable and the doll is strung with elastic. The original paper label on foot is marked, "Mickey Mouse, copy 1930 by Walter E. Disney." Mickey Mouse is inscribed on his stomach.

*Plate 48 -* **WOODEN MICKEY AND MINNIE MOUSE FIGURES** are five inches tall and made by the Fun-E-Flex Company. This variety has four-fingered hands. Minnie Mouse is wearing her original dress. Label is marked, "Walt E. Disney."

*Plate 49 -* **MICKEY MOUSE ASHTRAY** is made of metal. This rat-faced, black and white Mickey Mouse is very collectible.

*Plate 50 -* **MICKEY MOUSE FIGURAL STICKERS** come in their original box and are marked, "Walt Disney Enterprises."

*Plate 51 -* **MINNIE MOUSE CERAMIC ASH-TRAY** is marked "Walt Disney Enterprises" on the bottom and was made in Japan.

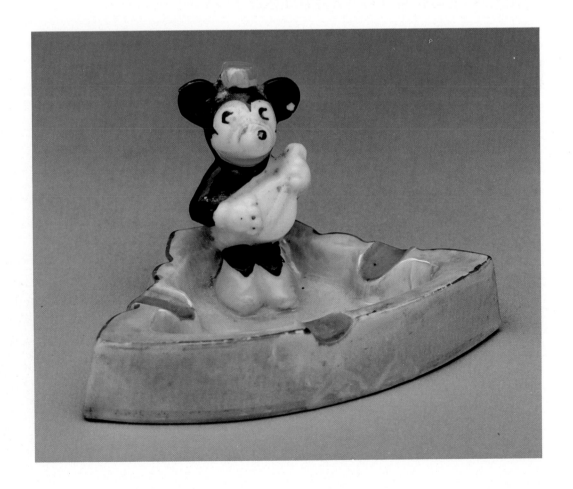

*Plate 52* - **Item A** - **MICKEY MOUSE CEREAL SPOON** was made by the Wm. Rogers Manufacturing Company.

**Item B** - **MICKEY MOUSE SILVER NAPKIN RING**

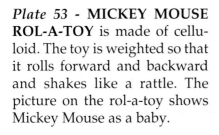

*Plate 53* - **MICKEY MOUSE ROL-A-TOY** is made of celluloid. The toy is weighted so that it rolls forward and backward and shakes like a rattle. The picture on the rol-a-toy shows Mickey Mouse as a baby.

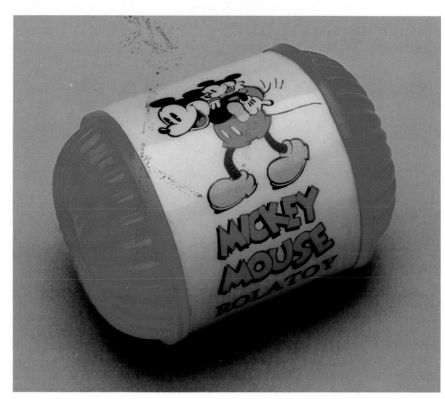

*Plate 54 -* **Item A - MICKEY MOUSE PENCIL HOLDER** is made by the Dixon Company. It is a composition figure, making it more rare than the pencil boxes.

**Item B - MICKEY MOUSE FOUNTAIN PEN** is made by the Inkograph Company and marked, "W.D.E." It is rare to have a complete decal.

*Plate 55 -* **MINNIE MOUSE BISQUE FIGU-RINE** is 5½ inches tall and made in Japan. Each bisque was individually hand painted.

*Plate 56* - Item A - MICKEY MOUSE PIN BACK BUTTONS

Item B - MICKEY MOUSE TIN CLICKER

Item C - MICKEY MOUSE COLA BOTTLE CAPS

*Plate 57* - **MICKEY MOUSE CHARM BRACELET** was made by Cohn & Rosenberg, Inc. They retailed from $.50 to $1.00. The bracelet features many of the early Disney characters.

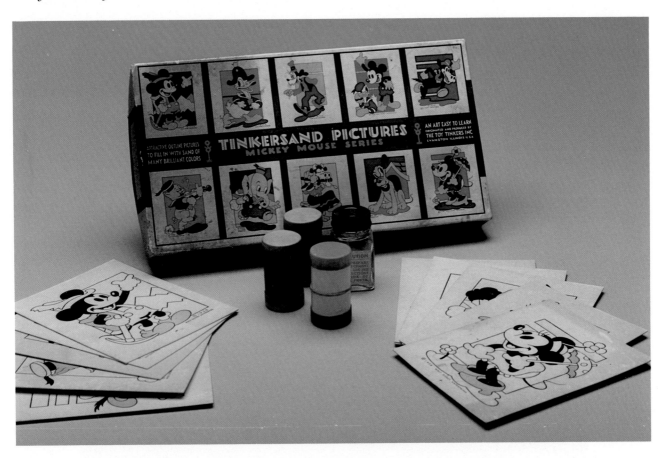

*Plate 58 -* **MICKEY MOUSE TINKERSAND PICTURES** were produced by the Toy Tinkers Inc. The pictures were created by gluing colored sand to the individual outline sheets.

*Plate 59 -***MICKEY MOUSE RUG** was manufactured by the Alexander Smith & Sons Company. They came in various sizes and a multitude of different scenes.

**Plate 60 - MICKEY MOUSE CHILD'S PLATE** is silverplated and was made by the International Silver Company.

**Plate 61 - MICKEY MOUSE FILM STORE DISPLAY** contained Cine Art Films made by the Hollywood Company for use in a Mickey Mouse projector.

*Plate 62* - **MICKEY MOUSE COMPACT** was made by Cohn & Rosenberger Company. It is made of enamel and tin and includes a mirror and compartment for powder inside. It's shown here with its original box which is in the shape of a book and marked, "c W.D."

*Plate 63* - **MICKEY MOUSE OLD MAID GAME** was made by the Whitman Company. The cards picture the earliest Disney characters. They are each individually marked, "W.D."

*Plate 64 -* **MICKEY MOUSE BASEBALL SET** is composed of three 3¼ inch tall bisque figurines each depicting a different baseball position. A smaller set does exist but it is hard to find a complete set.

*Plate 65 -* **MICKEY MOUSE WOODEN BLOCKS** were made by the Halsam Company. They are each marked, "c W.D."

***Plate 66 -* MICKEY AND MINNIE TOOTHBRUSH HOLDERS** are made of bisque and each has a movable arm which is connected to the figure by elastic. The two on the right are distinguished by their bulbous heads. The toothbrush pictured is actually one from the 1930's.

***Plate 67 -* MICKEY MOUSE BALLOON VENDOR** is a German tin wind-up. It was not a licensed Disney product but is collectible because of the small Mickey Mouse that the vendor holds. The hand lifts Mickey Mouse up and down when the toy is wound.

*Plate 68* - **RUBBER MICKEY MOUSE** was made by the Seiberling Latex Products Company of Akron, Ohio. Mickey Mouse is all rubber and measures 6 inches tall. This colorful version is the hardest to find.

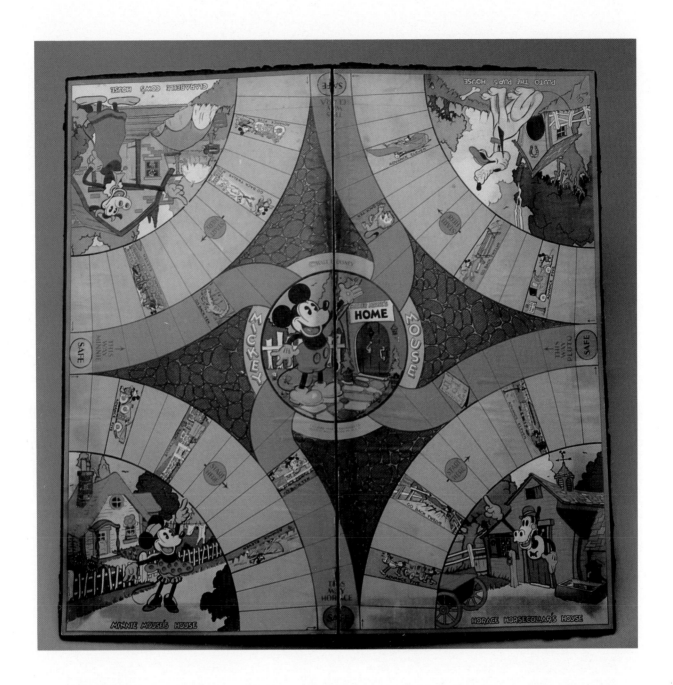

***Plate 69 -*** **MICKEY MOUSE GAME BOARD** is from the Marks Brothers game, "Coming Home."
Note the use of Horace Horsecollar and Clarabelle Cow, two of the earliest Disney characters.

*Plate 70* - **MICKEY MOUSE PENCIL BOXES** were all made by the Dixon Company. These are three different variations of pencil boxes children took to school with them each day.

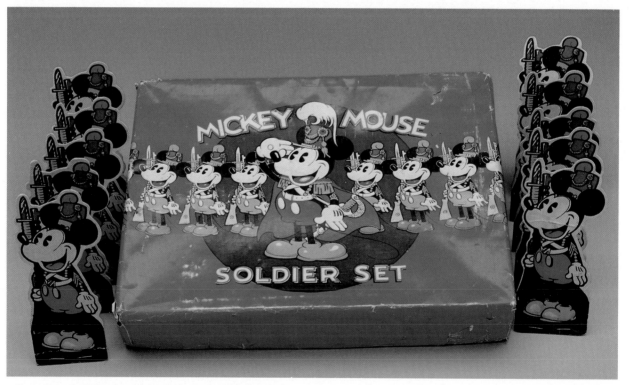

*Plate 71* - **MICKEY MOUSE SOLDIER SET** is made by Marks Brothers Company. The targets are made of heavy cardboard and are held up by wooden holders with slits to place the soldiers in. This is one of the many target sets marketed in the 1930's.

*Plate 72* - **MICKEY MOUSE DRUM** is made of tin by the Ohio Art Company. This is a nice example of early tin lithography.

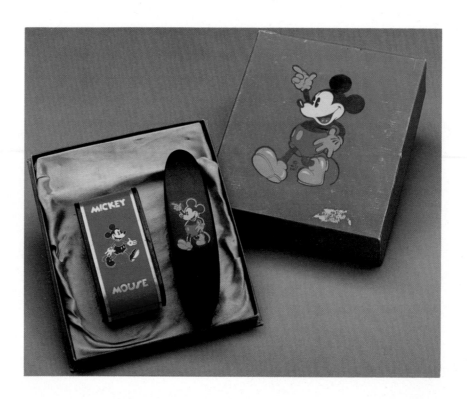

*Plate 73 -* **MICKEY MOUSE BRUSH SET** is made by Hughes Brush Company. The brush is wood with a red enamel plate wrapped around it.

*Plate 74 -* **MICKEY MOUSE PUPPET** appears to have been made from a pattern. The body and ears are a felt material.

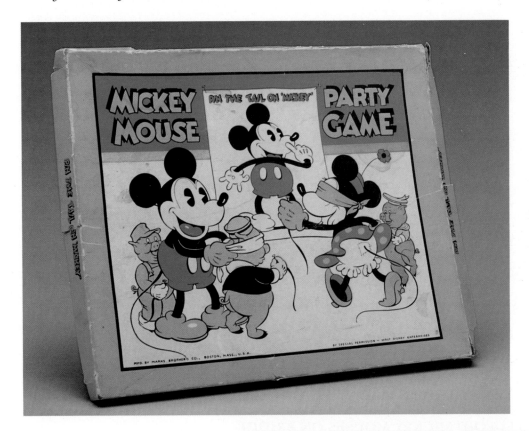

*Plate 75* - **MICKEY MOUSE PIN THE TAIL ON MICKEY PARTY GAME** was made by the Marks Brothers Company of Boston. The game includes Mickey Mouse paper poster and paper tails to be pinned.

*Plate 76* - **MICKEY MOUSE DOLLS** were manufactured by the Knickerbocker Toy Company. These are two different size variations of dolls produced. One is 11 inches with velvet shoes; the other is 12 inches tall with composition shoes.

*Plate 77* - **Item A - MICKEY MOUSE 1½ INCH TALL BISQUE FIGURINE**

**Item B - MICKEY MOUSE ON PLUTO BISQUE**

**Item C - CELLULOID MICKEY MOUSES ON BRIDGE**

*Plate 78 -* **MICKEY MOUSE NIGHT LIGHT** was made by the Micro-Lite Company. This "Kiddy-Lite" is battery operated. Mickey is made of pressed wood and marked, "c 1935 W.D. Ent." The base and light are made of tin.

*Plate 79* - **MICKEY MOUSE PARTY HORN** is made by Marks Brothers. The horn is made of heavy cardboard with the tip being made of wood.

***Plate 80 -* MICKEY MOUSE SPINNING TOP** was made by the Fritz Bueschel Company. It is all tin and the lithography is beautiful.

*Plate 81* - **MICKEY MOUSE PLAYING CARDS** were made by the Western P & L Company and copyrighted in 1932. Each card is individually marked, "Walt Disney Enterprises."

*Plate 82* - **MICKEY MOUSE FLIP MOVIE** was given away by the Dodge Car Company. This movie is titled "Mickey Takes Minnie for a Ride." The action is created by flipping the pages.

***Plate 83* - MICKEY MOUSE SNOW SHOVEL** was made by the Ohio Art Company. The shovel is tin and is marked, "c Walt Disney."

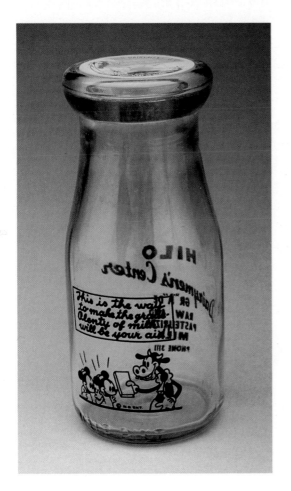

*Plate 84* - **MINNIE MOUSE FORK & SPOON HOLDER** was manufactured by the International Silver Company and given as baby gifts in the 1930's. Minnie Mouse is made of wood and the wheels make it movable. It is marked "W.D. Ent."

*Plate 85* - **MICKEY MOUSE MILK BOTTLE** by Hilo Dairymen's Center of Hawaii. Contained Gr"A"de raw and pasterized milk. The bottle is marked, "W.D. Ent."

*Plate 86* - **MICKEY MOUSE RUG** was made by the Alexander Smith & Sons Carpet Company. It highlights a great example of pie-eyed Mickey Mouse with Donald Duck.

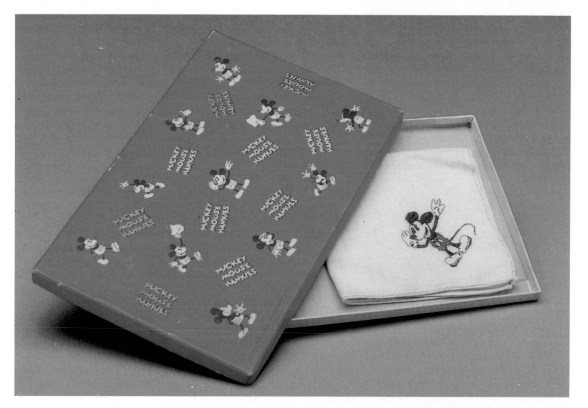

*Plate 87* - **MICKEY MOUSE HANKY** was made by the Herrmann Handkerchief Company. This handkerchief has a printed colorful design and shows original box.

**Plate 88 - MICKEY MOUSE TEA SET** was made in Japan and distributed by the George Borgfeldt Company. The box contains many colorful Disney graphics. Each piece of the set has a scene highlighting Mickey Mouse.

**Plate 89 - MINNIE MOUSE WOODEN FIGURE** is made by Fun-E-Flex and is 7 inches tall. Minnie Mouse has four-fingered hands and a rope-like tail.

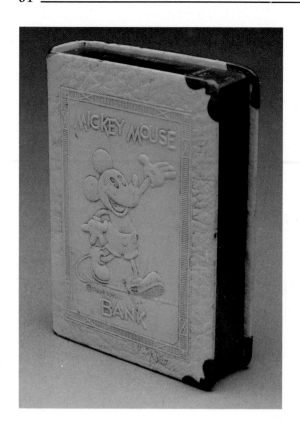

*Plate 90 -* **MICKEY MOUSE BOOK BANK** was released by the Zell Products Corp. and came with a key. Monies were deposited in a slot at the top.

*Plate 91 -* **MICKEY MOUSE WOODEN FIGURE** is thought to be the very first American-made Mickey Mouse toy. It is made of wood, leatherette and rope. When his tail is pushed down; his head bobs up. Mickey Mouse is 6¼ inches tall and is marked, "c 1928-1930 by Walter E. Disney." The feet on this figure are incorrect.

*Plate 92 -* **MICKEY MOUSE TELEPHONE BANK** was made by the N.N. Hill Brass Company. Mickey Mouse is made of hard cardboard and marked, "Walt Disney." The bank is attached to the back of the telephone.

*Plate 93 -* **MICKEY MOUSE WATERING CAN** was produced by the Ohio Art Company. It is made of tin and shows Mickey Mouse with a watering can.

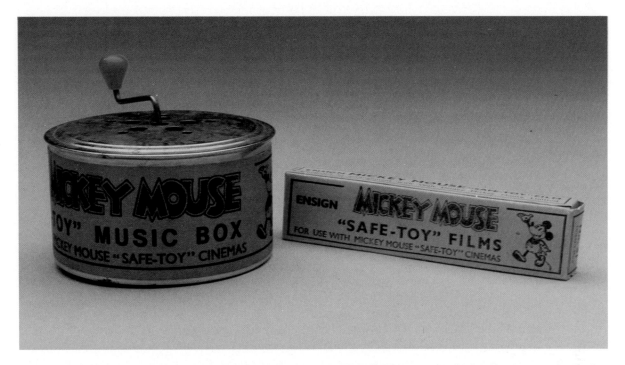

*Plate 94 -* **Item A - MICKEY MOUSE "TOY" MUSIC BOX** was made by Ensign and used to create the musical background when showing a "Safe-Toy" film. When the crank is turned, a musical tune is played.

**Item B - MICKEY MOUSE "SAFE-TOY"** film was made by Ensign Company of England. This film is titled "Mickey's Harp" and was used in the Ensign projector.

*Plate 95 -* **MICKEY MOUSE WATCH FOB** was used with an English pocket watch. Mickey Mouse is raised from the surface of the fob.

*Plate 96* - **Item A - MICKEY MOUSE WASH BOWL** is a lithographed tin item displaying scenes of Mickey and Minnie Mouse doing their wash.

**Item B - MICKEY MOUSE SPRINKLER** is the same tin lithography pattern. It is marked, "Walt Disney."

*Plate 97* - **MICKEY MOUSE SAND SIFTER** was made by the Ohio Art company. The piece was to be used by a child at the beach.

***Plate 98 -* MICKEY MOUSE HANDKERCHIEF** was made by the Herrmann Handkerchief Company and is pictured in the original box. A good example that Mickey Mouse was put on everything.

*Plate 99 -* **MICKEY MOUSE HALLOWEEN COSTUME** was used by trick or treaters in the 1930's. The costume covered every part of their bodies; it even came with a rubber tail.

# Long-billed Donald Duck

After the incredible success of Mickey Mouse, the Disney studios were in dire need of some new characters to interact with Mickey. On June 9, 1934, Donald Duck made his film debut in "The Wise Little Hen" and since that memorable date, has become a mainstay in the Disney stable of characters. He has appeared in over 128 cartoons and 42 various other shorts.

Donald Duck became the ideal foil for Mickey Mouse's new found righteousness. His antics were so engaging and were minus the discipline to which Mickey Mouse always had to adhere. Donald Duck did those things that Mickey Mouse couldn't because it might have tarnished his image. Donald Duck is Disney's most aggressive star. He is more like a duck in physical specifications and body than Mickey was a mouse or Goofy a dog.

Disney himself summed up Donald Duck: "Donald's got a big mouth, big belligerent eyes, a twistable neck and a substantial backside that's highly flexible. The duck comes near being the animator's ideal subject. He's got plasticity plus."

This chapter depicts Donald Duck from 1934-1937. Donald Duck from this period is identifiable by his long yellow bill and neck and his flat body. He is short and squatty with a waddling body. To indicate his mischievous nature one of his eyes was usually closed in a wink.

The super sensation that followed "The Wise Little Hen" propelled the same established merchandising machine that had mass-produced Mickey and Minnie Mouse to start churning out Donald Duck toys and items. Donald Duck quickly became Disney's second most famous character. Fewer Donald Duck items were created during the vintage years because production didn't begin until 1934 compared to Mickey Mouse's start in 1928.

The pictorial section on long-billed Donald Duck opens with a rare piece pictured in **Plate 100. Donald Duck and Minnie Mouse Acroba**t is a celluloid wind-up. It is very unusual to see a toy combining these two characters. Celluloid is rarely found in this type of condition because it was so brittle and highly flammable. The featherweight also contributed to the dents often found on celluloid toys. The box is also rare in that this box features complete "on box graphics" instead of a paper label glued to a brown box.

**Plate 101** shows the **Donald Duck with Pillar Toothbrush Holder**. This, in my experience, is the last one I needed to complete my set of toothbrush holders employing the characters of Mickey Mouse, Minnie Mouse, Donald Duck and Pluto. The toothbrush was placed in the pillar. This is a graphic representation of long-billed Donald Duck. All of the toothbrush holders were made in Japan and hand painted which accounts for varying colors on similar toothbrush holders.

The **Donald Duck and Pluto Handcar** pictured in **Plate 102** was produced by the Lionel Corporation. Included with the handcar was 72 inches of circular track. Along with the Mickey Mouse handcar, this train actually saved the Lionel Company from bankruptcy. To find a handcar with its original box can enhance the value. The key shown in the picture was used to wind the handcar up before it was placed in the track.

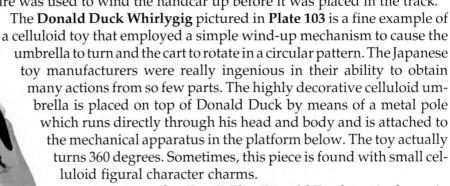

The **Donald Duck Whirlygig** pictured in **Plate 103** is a fine example of a celluloid toy that employed a simple wind-up mechanism to cause the umbrella to turn and the cart to rotate in a circular pattern. The Japanese toy manufacturers were really ingenious in their ability to obtain many actions from so few parts. The highly decorative celluloid umbrella is placed on top of Donald Duck by means of a metal pole which runs directly through his head and body and is attached to the mechanical apparatus in the platform below. The toy actually turns 360 degrees. Sometimes, this piece is found with small celluloid figural character charms.

A rare wooden **Fun-E-Flex Donald Duck** toy is shown in **Plate 104**. Both Donald Duck and the sled are made of wood and have the identifying Fun-E-Flex label on them marked, "Walt. Disney Enterprises." It is highly unusual to find a wooden character that is incorporated with another wooden object. The toy includes the original rope that was used to pull it.

The **Donald Duck** in **Plate 106** is a wind-up toy made in France. Donald is seven inches tall and waddles back and forth when wound. The movement simulates a duck's waddling perfectly. It was made of composition and aluminum.

**The Donald Duck Composition** doll in **Plate 107** is nine inches tall and was made by the Knickerbocker Toy Company. Donald Duck's head is movable and turns from side to side. He is pictured here with his original vest. Composition toys are a great find even for the advanced collector. Donald Duck is marked, "Walt Disney."

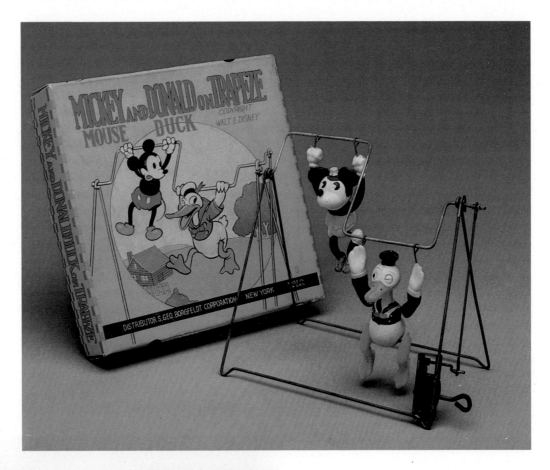

**Plate 100 - DONALD AND MINNIE ACRO-BAT** is a very rare celluloid wind-up toy. The combination of characters is one rarely seen. The box is also very rare featuring complete graphics instead of a paper label glued to a brown box. This piece was made in Japan and distributed by the George Borgfeldt Corporation.

**Plate 101 - DONALD DUCK TOOTHBRUSH HOLDER** is made of bisque and was hand painted in Japan. This is the hardest to find of all the character toothbrush holders. The toothbrush was placed in the pillar. This is a superb representation of long-billed Donald Duck.

*Plate 102* -**DONALD DUCK AND PLUTO HAND-CAR** was manufactured by the Lionel Corporation. Included with the train was 72 inches of circular track. It is hard to find the original ears on Pluto.

*Plate 103* - **DONALD DUCK WHIRLYGIG** - is a celluloid tin wind-up that moves in a circular movement when wound. The colorful balls are also made of celluloid. The umbrella spins as the tin cart moves.

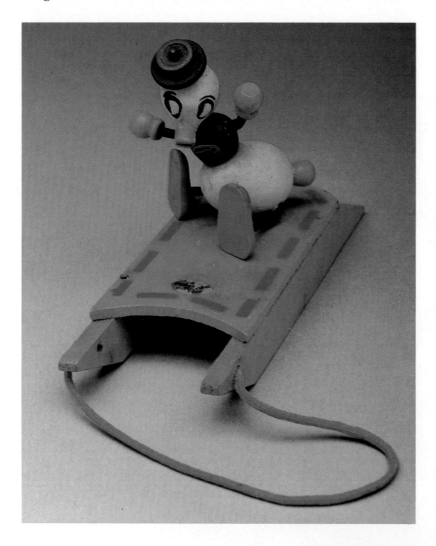

*Plate 104 -* **DONALD DUCK ON SLED** is a Fun-E-Flex product made of wood. Both the sled and Donald Duck have a label identifying them as Fun-E-Flex toys and marked, "Walt Disney Enterprises."

*Plate 105 -* **DONALD DUCK PULL TOY** was made by the Fisher Price Company. The toy is made of wood. The baton in Donald Duck's head moves up and down as the toy is pushed. It is marked, "W.D. Ent."

*Plate 106* - **DONALD DUCK WIND-UP** was manufactured in France. It is made of composition and aluminum and is seven inches tall.

***Plate 107 -* DONALD DUCK COMPOSITION DOLL** is 9 inches tall and was produced by the Knickerbocker Toy Company. Donald Duck is made of composition and has a movable head. He is wearing his original vest. It is marked, "Walt Disney" on back.

*Plate 108* - **Item A - DONALD DUCK HAIRBRUSH** made by the Hughes Company. The plate is enamel and marked, "W.D. Ent."

**Item B - DONALD DUCK PENCIL SHARPENER** is made of celluloid. The metal sharpener is encased in body.

*Plate 109* - **DONALD DUCK RUBBER FIGURE** is five inches tall and was produced by the Seiberling Latex Products Company. His head is movable. It is marked, "Walt Disney" on the back.

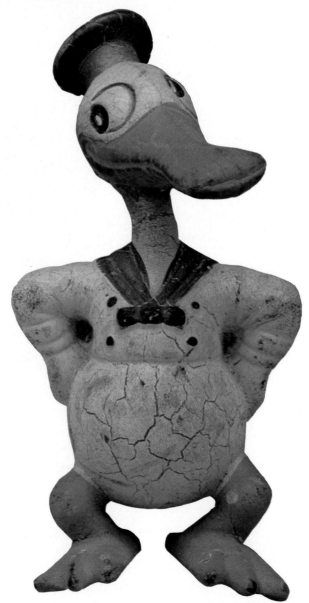

*Plate 110* - **Item A - DONALD DUCK MUSICIAN** is 4½" inches tall and made of bisque. This is the largest size for any Donald Duck Musician.

**Item B - DONALD DUCK BISQUE** is 4¾" inches tall.

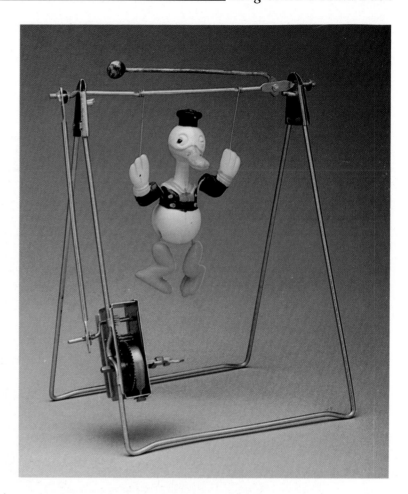

*Plate 111 -* **DONALD DUCK CARNIVAL FIGURE** is made of chalk and was given out at fairs as prizes during the 1930's.

*Plate 112 -* **DONALD DUCK ACROBAT** is a celluloid wind-up toy. Donald Duck is four inches tall and swings when toy is wound.

*Plate 113 -* Item A - **DONALD DUCK ENAMEL PIN**

**Item B - DONALD DUCK MINIATURE** is a 1½ inch tall bisque making it the smallest bisque produced.

**Item C - DONALD DUCK AND MICKEY MOUSE CELLULOID CHARMS**

*Plate 114 -* **DONALD DUCK UMBRELLAS** were made by the Louis Weiss Company. Pictured are two of the many variations produced.

*Plate 115* - **DONALD DUCK MUSICIAN BISQUES** are each four inches tall. This is a very hard to find set and many of the advanced bisque collectors are missing at least one of these.

*Plate 116* - **DISNEY CHALK FIGURES** were made in Japan and used as prizes or giveaways in various promotions.

*Plate 117 - DONALD DUCK TARGETS* are from the Marks Brothers Target Game. They are made of heavy cardboard. Each is individually marked, "Walt Disney Enterprises."

*Plate 118 - DONALD DUCK TOOTHBRUSH HOLDER* is made of bisque. The toothbrush was put in opening between Donald's hat and right hand.

# Friends from the Golden Age

This chapter includes some good friends of pie-eyed Mickey Mouse and long-billed Donald Duck. All items are from the 1930's - the "Golden Age" of Disneyana collectibles, and most are in great demand. There are many collectors who concentrate only on the Three Little Pigs or Snow White and The Seven Dwarfs memorabilia.

The Three Pigs were introduced during the Depression in 1933. They were first seen in the Silly Symphony cartoon film called "Three Little Pigs." It became the most famous cartoon featuring them.

The American public identified with the scared pigs and their continued search for security from the Big Bad Wolf. R.D. Feild said of the "Three Little Pigs" film: "No one will ever know to what extent the Three Little Pigs may be held responsible for pulling us out of the depression; but certainly the lyrical jeer at the Big Bad Wolf contributed not a little to the raising of people's spirits and to their defiance of circumstance!"

The public was so enthralled by the Three Little Pigs and the Big Bad Wolf that the same Disney merchandisers who were mass-producing Mickey Mouse and Donald Duck set their machines into motion and made many toys and novelties of the Three Little Pigs.

The pictorial section of "Friends from the Golden Age" starts with a bright colorful item pictured in **Plate 119**. The **Snow White Radio** was made by the Emerson Company which is still manufacturing radios today. The knobs are original and are referred to as "acorn" knobs. The radio itself is made of wood and each dwarf is carved out of the wood. It's really an eerie feeling plugging this radio in and having the rock and roll music of today blasting out.

The **Wooden Pluto** pictured in **Plate 120** was made by the Fun-E-Flex Company. The rariety of this piece is the wooden doghouse that came with Pluto. Pluto's ears are made of felt. The Fun-E-Flex label is located on top of Pluto's body. The **Pinocchio** pictured in **Plate 121** is the largest wooden figure of any character licensed by Disney. Pinocchio stands 19 inches tall and was manufactured by the Ideal Novelty and Toy Company. His hands and head are both made of composition. This piece really stands out when placed on a display shelf.

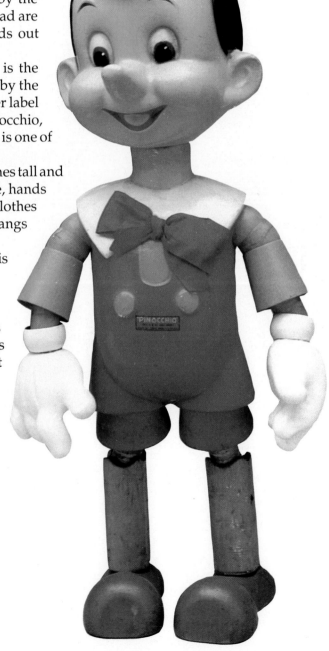

The **Wooden Pinocchio** pictured in **Plate 122** is the smallest wooden Pinocchio and the only one made by the Fun-E-Flex Company. He is 4¾ inches tall. The paper label found on the bottom of his foot is marked, "c Pinocchio, Walt Disney, Geo. Borgfeldt Corp. New York." This is one of the harder to find Fun-E-Flex pieces.

The **Dopey Doll** pictured in **Plate 123** is nine inches tall and made by the Knickerbocker Toy Company. His face, hands and shoes are made of composition. The original clothes are made of a velveteen material. The original tag hangs from Dopey's wrist.

The **Pinocchio Wind-Up** pictured in **Plate 124** is very unusual. He is totally made of composition with a very simple wind-up mechanism encased in his body. Pinocchio moves from side to side when wound. This is one of the largest wind-ups ever produced at 10½ inches high. The piece was made in Japan and distributed by the Borgfeldt Company. Another **Pinocchio Wind-up** is shown in **Plate 125**. **Pinocchio the Acrobat** was made by the Marx Company in 1939. Pinocchio's gyrations are incredible as he flips wildly when the base is set in motion. The lithography on the base is very colorful and bright and highlights many of the major characters from the movie.

*Plate 119 -* **SNOW WHITE RADIO** was made by Emerson Company which is still in business today. The knobs are original and referred to as "acorn knobs."

*Plate 120* - **WOODEN PLUTO** was manufactured by Fun-E-Flex. Pluto's ears are made of felt. Pluto is three inches wide. He is shown with the original dog house.

*Plate 121* - **PINOCCHIO** is made of wood by the Ideal Novelty & Toy Company. He is 19 inches tall making him the largest wooden figure licensed by Disney. The label on his stomach reads, "Dist. c By Walt Disney."

*Plate 122 -* **WOODEN PINOCCHIO** is 4¾ inches tall and made by the Fun-E-Flex Company in Japan. The paper label on his foot reads, "Pinocchio c Walt Disney, Geo Borgfeldt Corp., New York."

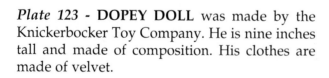

*Plate 123 -* **DOPEY DOLL** was made by the Knickerbocker Toy Company. He is nine inches tall and made of composition. His clothes are made of velvet.

*Plate 124 -* **PINOCCHIO WIND-UP** was distributed by Geo. Borgfeldt. He is made of composition and when wound moves back and forth. He is 10½ inches tall.

*Plate 125* - **PINOCCHIO THE ACRO-BAT** is a tin wind-up made by Marx Company. The piece is marked, "c 1939 Walt Disney Prod."

*Plate 126* - **CERAMIC FERDINAND THE BULL** was made by Brayton Pottery Company and is 2½ inches tall. The gold paper label on Ferdinand states "Copyright 1938 by Walt Disney Enterprises."

*Plate 127 - SNOW WHITE TEA SET* was manufactured by Aluminum Goods Company. Each of the toy utensils are made of aluminum and are rust proof. Included are pictorial Snow White napkins. The box is marked, "1937 Walt Disney Enterprises."

*Plate 128 - PLUTO AND MICKEY TOOTHBRUSH HOLDER* was hand painted in Japan. This is one of two toothbrush holders that include Pluto.

*Plate 129* - **THREE LITTLE PIGS CHINA,** is an excellent example of the fine colorful details of the graphics used on china produced in the 1930's.

*Plate 130* - **Item A - SNOW WHITE PLAYING CARDS** are marked, "W.D. Ent."

**Item B - SNOW WHITE METAL CHARM BRACELET**

**Item C - SNOW WHITE AND SEVEN DWARFS CELLULOID CHARMS**

**Plate 131- SNOW WHITE AND THE SEVEN DWARFS PICTURE PUZZLE** was made by the Whitman Publishing Company. The box is marked, "Walt Disney Enterprises."

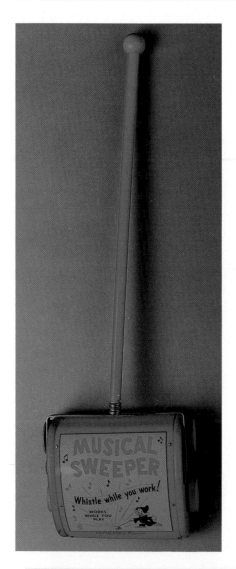

*Plate 132* - **DOPEY MUSICAL SWEEPER** was produced by the Fisher Price Company. When pushed, the sweeper plays, "Whistle While You Work."

*Plate 133* - **TORTOISE AND THE HARE RUG** was made in Italy and is very soft. A paper label on the back of the rug is marked, "By Permission Walt Disney."

*Plate 134 -* **DOPEY BANK** was made by the Crown Company and is made of composition. A metal latch is on the bottom of the bank.

*Plate 135 -* **SILLY SYMPHONY LIGHTS AND MICKEY MOUSE LIGHTS** were made by the Noma Light Company. Each light is enclosed in pictorial shades manufactured by Mazda.

*Plate 136 -* **WOODEN PLUTO** was made by the Fun-E-Flex Company. His ears are made of felt and he has a rope tail.

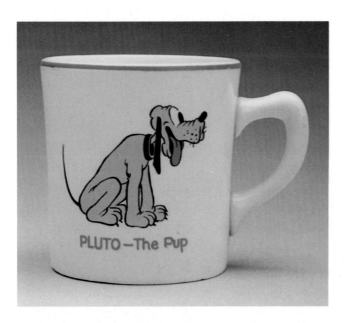

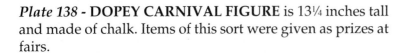

*Plate 137 -* **CERAMIC PLUTO MUG** was made by the Patriot China Company. It is the size of a coffee mug.

*Plate 138 -* **DOPEY CARNIVAL FIGURE** is 13¼ inches tall and made of chalk. Items of this sort were given as prizes at fairs.

*Plate 139* - **FERDINAND THE BULL COMPOSITION FIGURE** was made by the Knickerbocker Toy Company. Ferdinand's tail is made of rope and he normally has artificial flowers in his mouth.

*Plate 140 -* **SNOW WHITE AND THE SEVEN DWARFS BISQUE SET** were each hand painted in Japan and is the largest set made. Snow White is six inches tall and each Dwarf is five inches tall.

*Plate 141 -* **Item A - THREE LITTLE PIGS BISQUE SET**

**Item B - DIPPY THE GOOF BISQUE**

**Item C - FERDINAND BISQUE**

*Plate 142 -* **PINOCCHIO** was made by the Knickerbocker Toy Company and marked on the neck. Pinocchio is wood jointed, shown with his original clothes.

*Plate 143* - **THREE LITTLE PIGS CE-RAMIC MUG** was manufactured by the Patriot Company. It is marked, "Walt Disney."

*Plate 144* - **DOPEY DOLL** was produced by the Knickerbocker Toy Company and is 10 inches tall. His face is composition and his clothes are made of a velvet-like material.

*Plate 145 - **CERAMIC PLUTO**  was made by the Brayton Pottery Company. It is marked by a gold paper label.*

*Plate 146 - **FERDINAND THE BULL WIND-UP** is made of tin by the Marx Company. When wound, Ferdinand's tail goes round and round. The original cloth flower is in his mouth.*

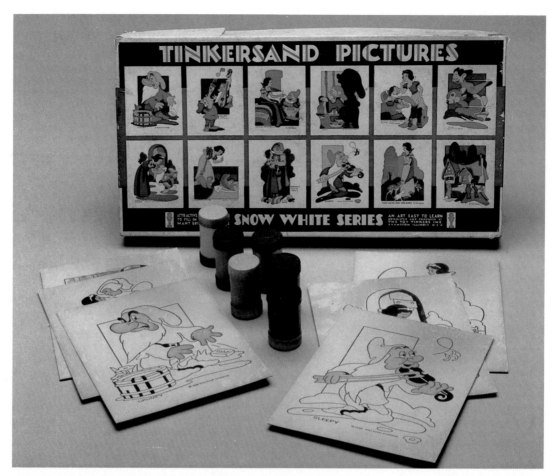

*Plate 147 -* **SNOW WHITE TINKERSAND PICTURES** were made by the Toy Tinkers, Inc. Individual pictures were made by applying colored sand with glue. Each is marked, "c 1938 Walt Disney Enterprises."

*Plate 148 -* **SNOW WHITE WAX FIGURINES** are each three inches tall and Snow White is 5¼ inches tall.

# Modern Merchandise

The final chapter of this book deals with Disney merchandise and memorabilia from 1940 to 1987. Earlier merchandise from this period is becoming highly collectible and the pieces are increasing almost daily. Most memorabilia from this period is affordable, but beware of 1960 and 1970 items; many dealers are asking higher prices than what the theme parks are charging for the same item.

The nostalgia market for the 1950's items is growing at a quick rate. Many collectors seek merchandise from feature films of this era — Davy Crockett, 1954; Lady and the Tramp, 1955 and Sleeping Beauty, 1959.

Most of the best 1950's merchandise is from the television show the Mickey Mouse Club. The show started on October 3, 1955. Mickey Mouse went from a movie star to a television star overnight. Mickey Mouse Club merchandise abounded in every imaginable item.

There are instant collectibles from the 1960's and 1970's that were produced on a limited run and are more valuable immediately after production. For example, the Schmid Company produces new sets yearly on a limited run. Many specialty items have been created for Mickey Mouse and Donald Duck's 50th birthdays. Collectors usually seek the different pins and buttons produced for special events at theme parks.

All items produced after September 29, 1938 are marked "WALT DISNEY PRODUCTIONS", "W.D.P.", "W.D. Co." or "Walt Disney Co." Dealers will not price items produced after this date in the same way. There were literally thousands of items produced during this era. A boxed item will appreciate in value much quicker than an identical item without the original box.

In this chapter, I have featured various merchandise of each decade after the "golden decade" of the 1930's. I have also featured the different prices that are based on the rareness and collectibility of the item.

The collecting of celluloids, which are paintings on celluloid by studio artists of an animated Disney character or object, is a different field of Disneyana collecting. Most animation art is priced very high and can be bought only through galleries specializing in animation or at auctions. Recently, a black and white celluloid and background from the cartoon "Orphan's Benefit" set a price record when it sold for $450,000.00 One should be very careful when purchasing any celluloid because they're not always what they're advertised to be. There are plenty of fakes and misrepresented "cels" on the market.

The best source for authenticating and appraising Disney cells is Ron Stark, who has established the S/R Laboratories. You can write him at:

Ron Stark
401 Falconrock Lane
Agoura, CA 91301

The later merchandise begins with two incredible celluloids from the movie, "Song of the South." **Plate 149** pictures a **celluloid on a Master Background.** A Master Background is an original painting created by artists from the studio and is actually photographed and used in the production of the final released version of the film. This means, that if you were to view the film, one would see this actual background somewhere during the film. A background painting serves as a setting in which the animated characters appear. "Song of the South" was produced in 1946. The Disney signature is authentic.

The celluloid pictured in **Plate 150** is referred to as a **Courvoisier or Courvoisier Style Background.** This is a background designed outside the studio for marketing and displaying the piece. Courvoisier Galleries of San Francisco was the agent for marketing the Walt Disney Studio's animation art until 1946. This "Song of the South" celluloid background was done with an airbrush to compliment the Brer Fox and Brer Rabbit celluloids. The signature of Walt Disney is authentic.

In **Plate 151** the **Marx Disney Television Playhouse** is shown. The playhouse, when assembled, can be used to simulate different scenes with Disney characters. Playsets are becoming increasingly more popular and desirable. The television playhouse comes with a script and includes appropriate props for the various scenes.

The **Bambi Ashtray** pictured in **Plate 152** was made by the Goebel Company; the same company

which manufactures the Hummel figurines. The marking on the bottom of the ashtray is marked with a stylized bee. It was made between 1957 and 1960. Earlier Goebel Disney figures are hard to find and are an excellent addition to any collection.

Two unauthorized **Mickey Mouse Brass Belt Buckles** are pictured in **Plate 153**. Even though all the embossed lettering is designed to give the impression that the rectangular buckle was made in the 1930's, it was actually manufactured in England in 1973. The exact manufacturing origin of this buckle is not known. The circular brass belt buckle insinuates that this was made by the Sun Rubber Company in 1937, but the Sun Rubber Company never made belt buckles. The buckle is not old, it began to be seen in the marketplace in 1971.

Store displays are becoming more and more desirable as they make great exhibits. The **Disney Character Store Display** in **Plate 154** was produced by the E.L.M. Toy Company to promote their handpainted Disney character figures. The **Disneykin Display** in **Plate 155** was made by the Marx Toy Company. It shows 34 different Disneykin characters. Each is made of plastic and is taken from various famous Disney cartoons.

The **Mickey Mouse Watch** pictured in **Plate 156** was made by the popular Timex Watch Company. It was manufactured for only one year and is electric, making it very unique. This is a watch that every serious Disney watch collector should own.

MICKEY MOUSE WALL WATCH
made by the Elgin Watch Company.

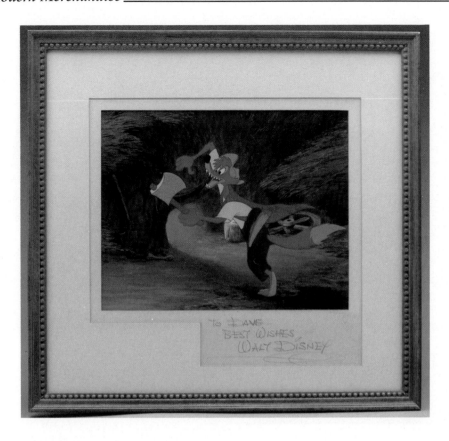

*Plate 149* - **SONG OF THE SOUTH CELLULOID** has the original master watercolor background used in the movie. It is an original painting created by studio artists and actually photographed and used in the production of the final, released version of the film.

*Plate 150* - **SONG OF THE SOUTH CELLULOID** has an airbrushed background, that was designed outside of the studio for marketing and display purposes only. Walt Disney's signature is authentic.

**Plate 151 - DISNEY TELEVISION PLAYHOUSE** was manufactured by the Marx Company. When assembled, the stage is set so that a play can be simulated using Disney's characters and scenes.

*Plate 152 - * **BAMBI ASHTRAY** was produced by the Goebel Company. It is marked with a stylized bee. Any Goebel Disney figurine is very desirable.

*Plate 153 -* **MICKEY MOUSE BELT BUCKLES** are both reproductions. Even though they appear to be made in the 1930's they surfaced in the marketplace in the early 1970's.

*Plate 154 -* **DISNEY CHARAC-TER STORE DISPLAY** was made by the E.L.M. Toy Company to promote their hand painted Disney character miniature figures.

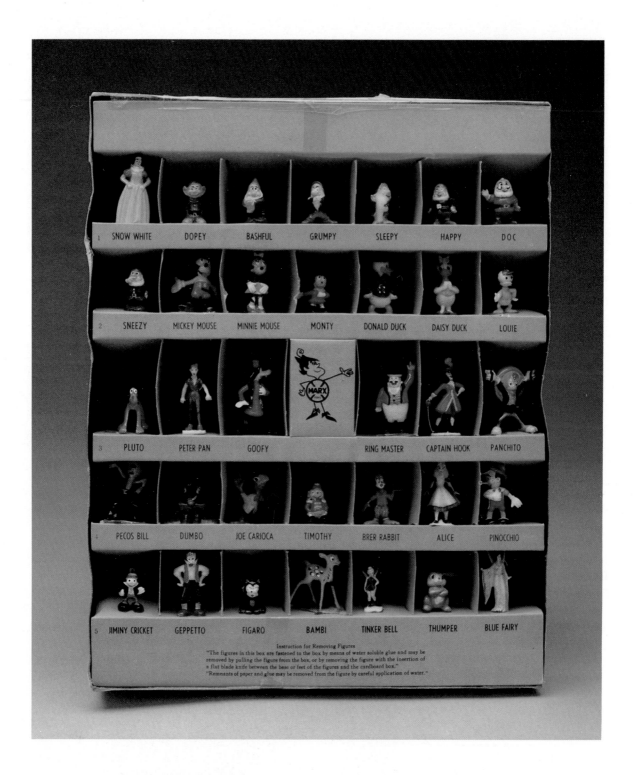

*Plate 155* - **DISNEYKIN DISPLAY** was made by the Marx Company. It displays 34 different Disneykins. Each are made of plastic and are from various famous Disney cartoons.

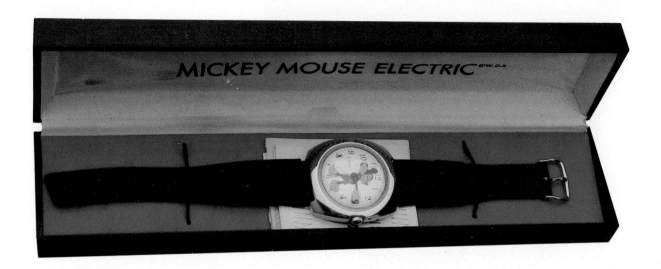

*Plate 156 -* **MICKEY MOUSE ELECTRIC WATCH** was made by the Timex Watch Company. This watch was made only one year — 1970.

*Plate 157 -* **DONALD DUCK CERAMIC FIGURINE** was made by the Evan K. Shaw company. It is four inches wide.

*Plate 158 - MICKEY MOUSE ALARM CLOCK* was made by Bayard in France. This clock was made in the 1970's and is a recreation of the clock Bayard distributed in the 1930's.

*Plate 159 - MICKEY MOUSE DISNEYKIN PLAY SET* was made by the Marx Company. The play sets always contain more than one character in a specific scene.

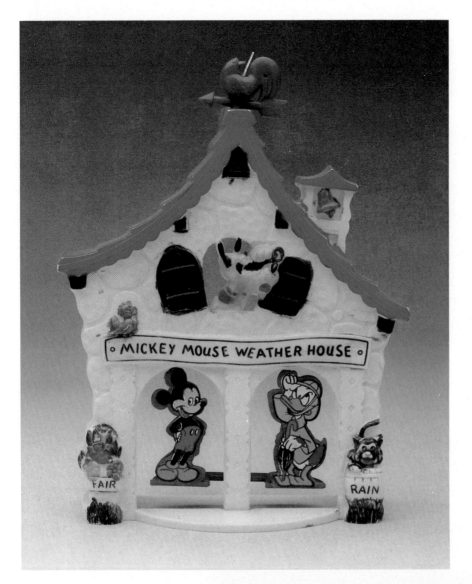

*Plate 160 - MICKEY MOUSE WEATHER HOUSE* was made by the Weatherman Company. The weather house is made of plastic.

*Plate 161 - THUMPER AND FLOWER CERAMIC FIGURES* were made by the Evan K. Shaw Company. Thumper is four inches tall and Flower is five inches tall.

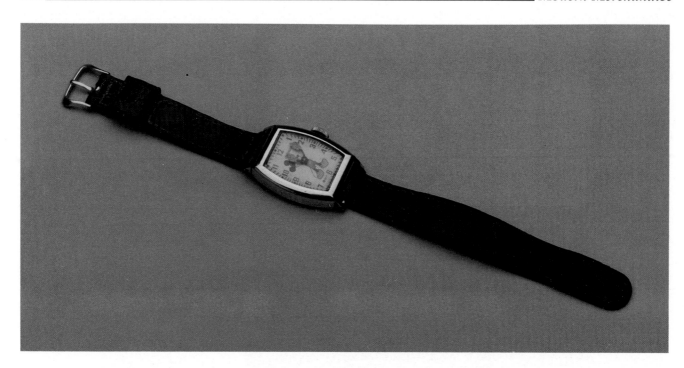

*Plate 162 -* **MICKEY MOUSE WATCH** was made by the U.S. Time Company. The rectangular face makes it unusual. The watch was made in 1946.

*Plate 163 -* **Item A - POOH'S HONEY CERAMIC BANK**

**Item B - PLUTO CARTOON PLASTIC SCISSORS**

***Plate 164 - DOC CLOCK*** was made by the Mi-Ken Company. His eyes move as the clock keeps time.

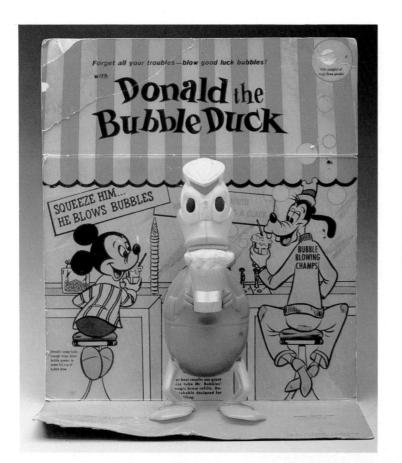

*Plate 165* - **DONALD THE BUBBLE DUCK** was made by Morris Plastic Corporation. Squeeze Donald Duck and he blows bubbles.

*Plate 166* - **DONALD DUCK JACK IN THE BOX** was made by the Spear Company. Donald Duck's head is composition and the clothes are felt.

*Plate 167* - **LUDWIG VON DRAKE CEL** is an original hand painted celluloid drawing actually used in a Walt Disney Production. The background is referred to as a "lithographed background." It is marked by a gold label on the back and released exclusively by Disneyland.

*Plate 168 -* **DISNEYKIN PLAY SETS** were made by the Marx Toy Company. Each depicts a separate scene. Many times the characters were not together in the movie depicted.

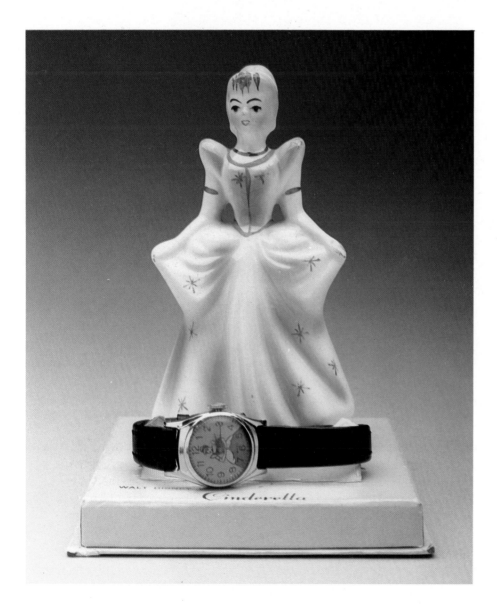

*Plate 169 -* **CINDERELLA WATCH** was made by the U.S. Time Company. Shown here is the original inside box display.

*Plate 170 -* **DISNEYANA** is a book by Cecil Munsey that is no longer in print. Copies of this book are sought after by every serious Disneyana collector.

*Plate 171* - **DISNEYKIN TV SCENES** are made by the Marx Toy Company and included only one character in each scene.

*Plate 172* - **DISNEY CHARACTERS FIGURINE** is one of the many products made annually by the Schmid Company. Many of the items are limited editions.

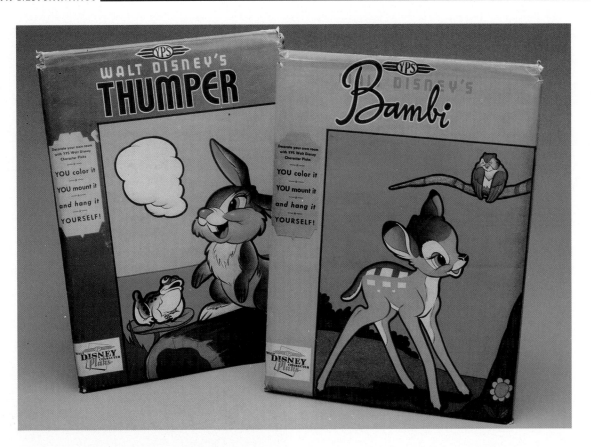

*Plate 173 -* **DISNEY WALL PLAQUES** were made by the Youngstown Pressed Steel Company. They are very colorful and made wonderful wall treatments for children's rooms.

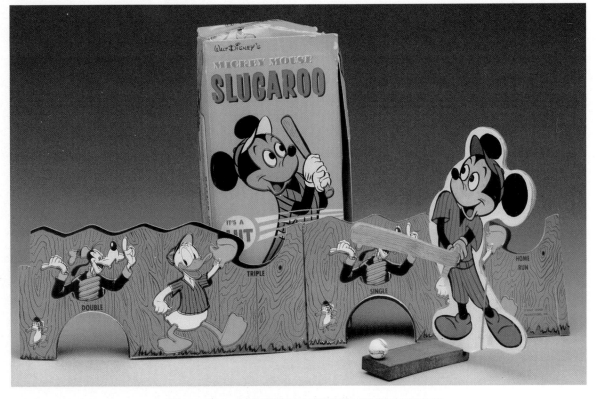

*Plate 174 -* **MICKEY MOUSE SLUGAROO**

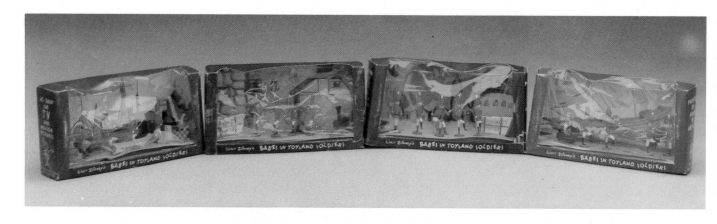

*Plate 175* - **BABES IN TOYLAND SOLDIER SETS** were made by the Marx Toy Company. There are six different sets in the series, each displaying a different scene from the "Babes in Toyland" movie.

*Plate 176* - **MICKEY AND MINNIE MOUSE SILVERWARE** are all modern steel-plated utensils.

*Plate 177 -* **MICKEY AND MINNIE MOUSE HAND PUPPETS** made by the Gund Company. The heads are made of rubber.

*Plate 178 -* **BAMBI DISNEYKIN** was made by the Marx Company and comes with original box which greatly adds to the value.

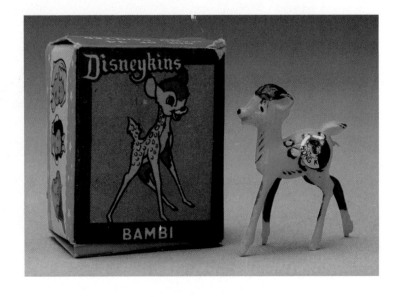

*Plate 179 -* **CERAMIC BAMBI FIGURINES** are seven inches long and were made by the American Pottery Company. They are marked by a stamp on the bottom of their stomachs.

*Plate 180 -* **DONALD DUCK PULL TOY** is completely made of wood by the Fisher Price Company. More modern Fisher Price toys have some plastic parts.

*Plate 181 -* **CASEY JUNIOR WALL DESIGN** is made of wood and was used in children's nurseries.

*Plate 182* - **Item A** - **MICKEY MOUSE DOLL** was made by the Horsman Doll Company.

**Item B** - **TIN SPINNING TOP**

**Item C** - **DISNEYLAND BUTTON**

*Plate 183* - **A CELEBRATION OF COMIC ART AND MEMORABILIA,** by Robert Lesser, is an excellent reference book on comic toys. This book has been out of print so it too has become collectible.

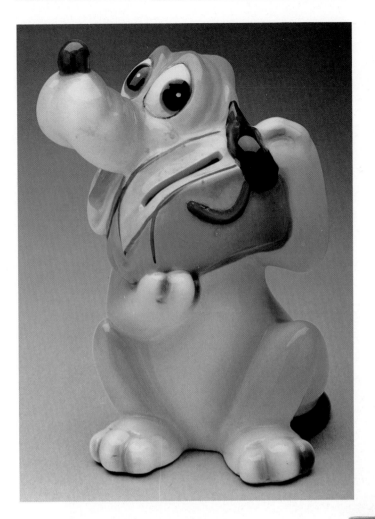

*Plate 184* - **PLUTO CERAMIC BANK** was produced by the Leeds China Company.

*Plate 185* - **ROLYKINS** were made by the Marx Toy Company. They utilize ball bearings to loop and zoom. These were made of many different Disney characters.

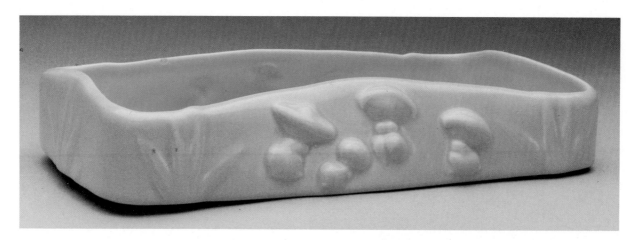

*Plate 186 -* **MUSHROOM CERAMIC BOWL** was manufactured by the Vernon Kilns Company. It is from the movie, "Fantasia."

*Plate 187 -* Item A - **MICKEY TIN MOUSEKABANK**

Item B - **MICKEY MOUSE PEZ DISPENSER**

Item C - **MICKEY MOUSE CARD GAME**

*Plate 188 -* **Item A - DONALD DUCK PLASTIC WIND-UP** made by Marx.

**Item B - GOOFY PLASTIC WIND-UP** made by Marx. The chipmunk revolves clockwise when wound.

*Plate 189 -* **MICKEY MOUSE DOLLS** made by the Horsman Doll Company. Mickey Mouse is made of rubber with bendable limbs.

*Plate 190 -* **MICKEY MOUSE PLASTIC FIGURES**

*Plate 191 -* **Item A - DANCING MICKEY DEVICE**
**Item B - RUBBER GOOFY**
**Item C - SCROOGE McDUCK TREASURE CHEST BANK**

*Plate 192 -* **CASEY JUNIOR DISNEYLAND EXPRESS TRAIN** made by the Marx Toy Company. The train is a tin wind-up.

*Plate 193 -* **MICKEY MOUSE RUG** measures 35 inches by 20 inches.

*Plate 194 -* **MICKEY MOUSE WALL WATCH** *-* was made by the Elgin Watch Company. It is 38 inches tall and used as a wall decoration.

*Plate 195 -* **BIG BAD WOLF DOLL** *-* was manufactured by the Gund Company.

*Plate 196 -* **PIPSQUEAKS** are made by Marx. Push the character's head in and watch them squeak.

*Plate 197 -* **CHRISTMAS 1980 PLATE** by Schmid.

*Plate 198 -* **MICKEY MOUSE PLASTIC RADIO**

*Plate 199* - PLASTIC DONALD DUCK BATH TOY

*Plate 200* -**MICKEY MOUSE CERAMIC CANDY CONTAINER** is marked, "1961 Walt Disney Productions."

*Plate 210* - **MICKEY MOUSE BOTTLE WARMER** was made by the Hankscraft Company.

*Plate 202* - Item A - MICKEY MOUSE PLASTIC MEGAPHONE

Item B - DONALD DUCK CERAMIC CUP

*Plate 203*- Item A - RUBBER TINKER BELL

Item B - PLASTIC SNOW WHITE used with watch purchase.

Item C - RUBBER MICKEY MOUSE

*Plate 204 - **MICKEY MOUSE LAMP** is marked, "Walt Disney Productions."* Mickey Mouse is rubber and the shade is a parchment-like material

*Plate 205* - **DISNEY SOAK-IES** are made by the Colgate Palmolive Company. Each contains bubble bath.

*Plate 206* - **NEW DISNEYKINS PLAY SETS** were made by Marx. They are more rare than the Disneykin Play Sets and command a much higher price.

*Plate 207 -*
**MICKEY MOUSE
PLASTIC BANKS**

*Plate 208 -* **MICKEY MOUSE AND DONALD DUCK RUBBER FIGURES**

*Plate 209 -* **DISNEY PUZZLE BLOCKS**

*Plate 210 -* **DONALD DUCK TIN TEA SET** was made by the Ohio Art Company in the early 1940's.

*Plate 212* - **Item A - AVON MICKEY MOUSE CONTAINER**

**Item B - RUBBER MICKEY MOUSE**

**Item C - PLASTIC MINNIE MOUSE FIGURINE**

*Plate 212* - **MICKEY MOUSE CLUB LUNCH BOX** was made by Aladdin Industries.

*Plate 213 -* **BAMBI CERAMIC PLANTER** was made by the Leeds China Company and marked "Walt Disney Prod."

*Plate 214 -* **Item A -** **MICKEY MOUSE WATCH** made by U.S. Time.

**Item B -** **MICKEY & MINNIE MOUSE TENNIS WATCH**

**Item C -** **SNOW WHITE U.S. TIME WATCH**

**Item D -** **MICKEY MOUSE BRADLEY POCKET WATCH**

*Plate 215* - Item A - DONALD DUCK TRICKY TOE TOY

Item B - GOOFY BALL TOY

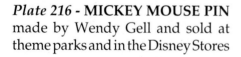

*Plate 216* - **MICKEY MOUSE PIN** made by Wendy Gell and sold at theme parks and in the Disney Stores

*Plate 217 - * **MICKEY AND MINNIE MOUSE RUB-BER DOLLS** by Dakin.

*Plate 218 - * **MICKEY MOUSE RUG**

*Plate 219 -* **MICKEY AND MIN-NIE MOUSE TIN TEA SET**

*Plate 220 -* **FIRE FIGHTERS DOME LUNCH BOX** made by Aladdin Industries.

Plate 221 - Item A - MICKEY MOUSE GUMBALL MA-CHINE

Item B - MICKEY MOUSE PLASTIC BANK

Plate 222 - Item A - MICKEY MOUSE MUSIC MAKER

Item B - MICKEY MOUSE MOVING TOY

*Plate 223* - Item A - MICKEY MOUSE PLASTIC NODDER

Item B - MICKEY MOUSE SUN RUBBER BALL

*Plate 224* - MICKEY MOUSE
CANDY TIN

*Plate 225 - MICKEY MOUSE HARD RUBBER FIGURE*

*Plate 226 - Item A - MICKEY MOUSE FLASHLIGHT* by Arco.

**Item B - MICKEY MOUSE LITTLE TREASURES** by Mattel.

*Plate 227* - MICKEY'S MUSICAL MONEY BOX

*Plate 228* - MICKEY MOUSE PLATES

# Price Guide

The price guide for Disneyana collectibles is to be used as a point of reference before buying or selling an item. Any price guide tends to be subjective in nature, and I've used the sources available to me to arrive at what I think are accurate price points in today's marketplace. This Disney toy market can change dramatically in a very short span of time.

I have determined the prices for each item based on a number of factors and sources:

1. What I paid for each item.
2. Auction catalogs.
3. Mail auction price realized lists.
4. Toy and doll show prices.
5. Antique Trader ads.

I feel the prices suggested are excellent estimations of what each item is actually worth. The basic law of economics: supply and demand, can shoot holes through any price guide. The adage that the worth of a toy is what someone will pay for it is still prevalent for today's collectors.

Emotion and the strong desire of wanting to add a certain piece to your collection will result in paying more.

The following descriptions relate to the condition of the toy and how they are priced accordingly.

## GOOD CONDITION

The toy is in working order, has been used, shows general wear and tear. The toy must look fairly clean with little or no rust.

## EXCELLENT, MINT CONDITION

The toy is clean and looks as if it was never used. It is complete and all functions are operative. Mint applies to mint in the box (MIB) and means the toy is in its original package. In many cases, the box is worth more than the item itself.

### Pie-eyed Mickey & Minnie Mouse

| Plate # | Good | Excellent Mint |
|---|---|---|
| 1) - Mickey Mouse On Pluto | $3,500.00 | $4,000.00 |
| 2) - Hobby Horse Mickey Mouse | $1,500.00 | $2,000.00 |
| 3) - Rag Doll Mickey Mouse 5" | $500.00 | $700.00 |
| 4) - Rag Doll Mickey Mouse 8" | $550.00 | $725.00 |
| 5) - Cowboy Mickey Mouse Doll | $3,000.00 | $3,500.00 |
| 6) - Mickey Mouse 7" Steiff Doll | $2,000.00 | $2,500.00 |
| 7) - Mickey Mouse 9" Steiff Doll | $2,500.00 | $3,000.00 |
| 8) - Mickey Mouse 11" Steiff Doll | $2,800.00 | $3,300.00 |
| 9) - Mickey Mouse English Pocket Watch | $2,000.00 | $2,500.00 |
| 10) - Two Pals Boxed Bisque Set | $1,000.00 | $1,500.00 |
| 11) - Musician Boxed Bisque Set | $1,200.00 | $1,600.00 |
| 12) - Mickey Mouse Lunch Kit | $2,500.00 | $3,000.00 |
| 13) - Mickey Mouse Circus Train | $8,500.00 | $10,000.00 |
| 14) - Mickey Mouse Oil Drum Lid | $1,000.00 | $1,200.00 |
| 15) - Mickey Mouse Electric Lamp/Shade | $1,500.00 | $2,000.00 |
| 16) - Mickey Mouse Lamp Filament | $400.00 | $450.00 |

| Plate # | Good | Excellent Mint |
|---|---|---|
| 17) - Mickey Mouse Porringer | $550.00 | $600.00 |
| 18) - Mickey Mouse Alarm Clock | $1,000.00 | $1,400.00 |
| 19) - Mickey Mouse Alarm Clock | $1,000.00 | $1,400.00 |
| 20) - Mickey Mouse In Canoe Bisque | $2,000.00 | $2,500.00 |
| 21) - German Mickey Maus | $300.00 | $350.00 |
| 22) - Wooden Balancing Mickey Mouse | $1,200.00 | $1,600.00 |
| 23) - Mickey Mouse Mystery Tunnel | $850.00 | $900.00 |
| 24) - Mickey Mouse Mystery Tunnel | $850.00 | $900.00 |
| 25) - Mickey & Minnie Mouse Piano | $1,800.00 | $2,300.00 |
| 26) - Mickey Mouse Whirlygig | $2,500.00 | $3,000.00 |
| 27) - Mickey Mouse Bagatelle | $500.00 | $650.00 |
| 28) - Mickey Mouse Movie Jector | $600.00 | $700.00 |
| 29) - Mickey Mouse Pencil Box | $125.00 | $150.00 |
| 30) - Mickey Mouse Washing Machine | $500.00 | $525.00 |
| 31) - Mickey Mouse Target Game | $400.00 | $450.00 |
| 32) - Mickey Mouse Toy Slides | $50.00 | $65.00 |
| 33) - Minnie Mouse Silver Cup | $60.00 | $70.00 |

| Plate # | Good | Excellent Mint |
|---|---|---|
| 34) - Minnie Mouse Trapeze | $700.00 | $750.00 |
| 35) - Mickey Mouse Cane | $200.00 | $250.00 |
| 36) - Mickey Mouse Lights | $250.00 | $300.00 |
| 37) - Mickey Mouse Figural Pencil Box | $400.00 | $425.00 |
| 38) - Mickey Mouse Tea Set | $500.00 | $575.00 |
| 39) - Mickey Mouse China Tea Set | $525.00 | $600.00 |
| 40) - Mickey Mouse Tamborine & Guitar | $400.00 | $500.00 |
| 41) - Mickey Mouse Bells | $200.00 | $225.00 |
| 42) - Mickey & Minnie Mouse Dolls | $200.00 | $250.00 |
| 43) - Mickey & Minnie Mouse Dolls | $200.00 | $250.00 |
| 44) - Item A - Mickey Printing Blocks | $50.00 | $60.00 |
| Item B - Mickey Mouse On Bridge | $175.00 | $200.00 |
| 45) - Minnie Mouse Pin Cushion | $700.00 | $750.00 |
| 46) - Mickey Mouse Knickerbocker Doll | $2,000.00 | $2,500.00 |
| 47) - Item A - Mickey Mouse Sharpener | $300.00 | $375.00 |
| Item B - Mickey Mouse Nursery Doll | $400.00 | $450.00 |
| 48) - Mickey & Minnie Mouse Figures | $425.00 | $475.00 |
| 49) - Mickey Mouse Ashtray | $600.00 | $750.00 |
| 50) - Mickey Mouse Figural Stickers | $100.00 | $110.00 |
| 51) - Minnie Mouse Ceramic Ashtray | $250.00 | $275.00 |
| 52) - Item A - Mickey Mouse Cereal Spoon | $50.00 | $60.00 |
| Item B - Mickey Mouse Napkin Ring | $55.00 | $75.00 |
| 53) - Mickey Mouse Rol-A-Toy | $400.00 | $450.00 |
| 54) - Item A - Mickey Mouse Pencil Holder | $400.00 | $425.00 |
| Item B - Mickey Mouse Fountain Pen | $150.00 | $175.00 |
| 55) - Minnie Mouse Bisque Figurine | $425.00 | $475.00 |
| 56) - Item A - Mickey Mouse Buttons | $50.00 | $55.00 |
| Item B - Mickey Mouse Tin Clicker | $50.00 | $55.00 |
| Item C - Mickey Mouse Bottle Tops | $15.00 | $20.00 |
| 57) - Mickey Mouse Charm Bracelet | $100.00 | $125.00 |
| 58) - Mickey Mouse Tinkersand Pictures | $100.00 | $125.00 |
| 59) - Mickey Mouse Rug | $350.00 | $400.00 |
| 60) - Mickey Mouse Child's Plate | $100.00 | $125.00 |
| 61) - Mickey Mouse Film Store Display | $400.00 | $450.00 |
| 62) - Mickey Mouse Compact | $700.00 | $750.00 |
| 63) - Mickey Mouse Old Maid Game | $60.00 | $75.00 |
| 64) - Mickey Mouse Baseball Set | $750.00 | $800.00 |
| 65) - Mickey Mouse Wooden Blocks | $60.00 | $65.00 |
| 66) - Mickey & Minnie Mouse Holders | $300.00 | $325.00 |
| 67) - Mickey Mouse Balloon Vendor | $700.00 | $725.00 |
| 68) - Seiberling Rubber Mickey Mouse | $200.00 | $225.00 |
| 69) - Mickey Mouse Game Board | $20.00 | $25.00 |
| 70) - Mickey Mouse Pencil Boxes | $125.00 | $150.00 |
| 71) - Mickey Mouse Soldier Set | $375.00 | $400.00 |
| 72) - Mickey Mouse Tin Drum | $200.00 | $225.00 |
| 73) - Mickey Mouse Brush Set | $125.00 | $150.00 |
| 74) - Mickey Mouse Puppet | $225.00 | $250.00 |
| 75) - Mickey Mouse Pin The Tail Game | $95.00 | $110.00 |
| 76) - Mickey Mouse Knickerbocker Dolls | $400.00 | $500.00 |
| 77) - Item A - Mickey Mouse Bisque | $90.00 | $95.00 |
| Item B - Mickey Mouse/Pluto Bisque | $75.00 | $100.00 |
| Item C - Mickey Mouses On Bridge | $200.00 | $250.00 |
| 78) - Mickey Mouse Night Light | $400.00 | $450.00 |
| 79) - Mickey Mouse Party Horn | $90.00 | $100.00 |
| 80) - Mickey Mouse Spinning Top | $300.00 | $325.00 |
| 81) - Mickey Mouse Playing Cards | $50.00 | $75.00 |
| 82) - Mickey Mouse Flip Movie | $50.00 | $60.00 |
| 83) - Mickey Mouse Snow Shovel | $200.00 | $250.00 |
| 84) - Minnie Mouse Fork & Spoon Holder | $600.00 | $650.00 |
| 85) - Mickey Mouse Milk Bottle | $150.00 | $175.00 |

| Plate # | Good | Excellent Mint |
|---|---|---|
| 86) - Mickey Mouse Rug | $300.00 | $325.00 |
| 87) - Mickey Mouse Hanky | $200.00 | $225.00 |
| 88) - Mickey Mouse China Tea Set | $350.00 | $400.00 |
| 89) - Minnie Mouse Wooden Figure | $700.00 | $750.00 |
| 90) - Mickey Mouse Book Bank | $100.00 | $110.00 |
| 91) - Mickey Mouse Wooden Figure | $1,500.00 | $2,000.00 |
| 92) - Mickey Mouse Telephone Bank | $400.00 | $425.00 |
| 93) - Mickey Mouse Watering Can | $250.00 | $275.00 |
| 94) - Item A - Mickey Mouse Music Box | $200.00 | $225.00 |
| Item B - Mickey Mouse Film | $30.00 | $35.00 |
| 95) - Mickey Mouse English Watch Fob | $150.00 | $165.00 |
| 96) - Item A - Mickey Mouse Wash Bowl | $200.00 | $225.00 |
| Item B - Mickey Mouse Sprinkler | $150.00 | $165.00 |
| 97) - Mickey Mouse Sand Sifter | $225.00 | $250.00 |
| 98) - Mickey Mouse Handerchief | $250.00 | $300.00 |
| 99) - Mickey Mouse Halloween Costume | $500.00 | $550.00 |

### Long-billed Donald Duck

| Plate # | Good | Excellent Mint |
|---|---|---|
| 100) - Donald Duck & Minnie Mouse | $2,200.00 | $3,000.00 |
| 101) - Donald Duck Toothbrush Holder | $1,200.00 | $1,500.00 |
| 102) - Donald Duck & Pluto Handcar | $1,800.00 | $2,300.00 |
| 103) - Donald Duck Whirlygig | $2,000.00 | $2,500.00 |
| 104) - Donald Duck On Sled | $1,800.00 | $2,000.00 |
| 105) - Fisher Price Donald Duck Pull Toy | $225.00 | $250.00 |
| 106) - Donald Duck Wind-Up | $450.00 | $500.00 |
| 107) - Donald Duck Composition Doll | $1,500.00 | $1,800.00 |
| 108) - Item A - Donald Duck Hairbrush | $75.00 | $85.00 |
| Item B - Donald Duck Sharpener | $275.00 | $300.00 |
| 109) - Seiberling Rubber Donald Duck | $250.00 | $300.00 |
| 110) - Item A - Donald Duck Musician | $275.00 | $300.00 |
| Item B - Donald Duck Bisque | $400.00 | $425.00 |
| 111) - Donald Duck Carnival Figure | $100.00 | $125.00 |
| 112) - Donald Duck Acrobat | $500.00 | $700.00 |
| 113) - Item A - Donald Duck Enamel Pin | $85.00 | $95.00 |
| Item B - Donald Duck 1½" Bisque | $100.00 | $110.00 |
| Item C - Celluloid Charms | $20.00 | $25.00 |
| 114) - Donald Duck Umbrellas | $175.00 | $200.00 |
| 115) - Donald Duck Musician Bisque Sets | $1,500.00 | $1,800.00 |
| 116) - Donald Duck Chalk Figures | $50.00 | $75.00 |
| 117) - Donald Duck Targets | $15.00 | $20.00 |
| 118) - Donald Duck Toothbrush Holder | $275.00 | $300.00 |

### Friends from the Golden Age

| Plate # | Good | Excellent Mint |
|---|---|---|
| 119) - Snow White Radio | $2,800.00 | $3,500.00 |
| 120) - Wooden Fun-E-Flex Pluto | $350.00 | $400.00 |
| 121) - Ideal Novelty's Wooden Pinocchio | $750.00 | $900.00 |
| 122) - Fun-E-Flex Wooden Pinocchio | $200.00 | $225.00 |
| 123) - Dopey Doll | $200.00 | $225.00 |
| 124) - Pinocchio Wind-Up | $350.00 | $400.00 |
| 125) - Pinocchio The Acrobat | $400.00 | $450.00 |
| 126) - Ceramic Ferdinand the Bull | $125.00 | $150.00 |
| 127) - Snow White Tin Tea Set | $275.00 | $300.00 |
| 128) - Pluto & Mickey Mouse Holder | $300.00 | $325.00 |
| 129) - Three Little Pigs China | $250.00 | $300.00 |
| 130) - Item A - Snow White Playing Cards | $35.00 | $40.00 |
| Item B - Snow White Charm Bracelet | $100.00 | $120.00 |
| Item C - Snow White Charms | $30.00 | $35.00 |
| 131) - Snow White Picture Puzzle | $60.00 | $70.00 |
| 132) - Dopey Musical Sweeper | $125.00 | $150.00 |
| 133) - Tortoise And The Hare Rug | $150.00 | $200.00 |
| 134) - Crown's Dopey Bank | $175.00 | $200.00 |
| 135) - Silly Symphony Lights | $200.00 | $225.00 |

| Plate # | Good | Excellent Mint | Plate # | Good | Excellent Mint |
|---|---|---|---|---|---|
| *136)* - Large Wooden Fun-E-Flex Pluto | $325.00 | $350.00 | *188)* - Item A - Donald Duck Wind-Up | $80.00 | $85.00 |
| *137)* - Ceramic Pluto Mug | $100.00 | $110.00 | Item B - Goofy Plastic Wind-Up | $90.00 | $100.00 |
| *138)* - Dopey Carnival Figure | $80.00 | $100.00 | *189)* - Mickey Mouse Dolls | $15.00 | $20.00 |
| *139)* - Composition Ferdinand The Bull | $120.00 | $140.00 | *190)* - Mickey Mouse Plastic Figures | $10.00 | $15.00 |
| *140)* - Snow White & 7 Dwarfs Bisque Set | $600.00 | $650.00 | *191)* - Item A - Dancing Mickey Mouse | $5.00 | $10.00 |
| *141)* - Item A - Three Little Pigs Bisque Set | $175.00 | $200.00 | Item B - Rubber Goofy | $5.00 | $10.00 |
| Item B - Goofy The Goof Bisque Set | $50.00 | $65.00 | Item C - Scrooge McDuck | | |
| Item C - Ferdinand The Bull Bisque | $50.00 | $65.00 | Treasure Bank | $35.00 | $40.00 |
| *142)* - Knickerbocker Pinocchio | $350.00 | $400.00 | *192)* - Casey Jr. Disneyland Express | $65.00 | $70.00 |
| *143)* - Three Little Pigs Ceramic Mug | $75.00 | $80.00 | *193)* - Mickey Mouse Rug | $150.00 | $200.00 |
| *144)* - Knickerbocker Dopey Doll | $150.00 | $175.00 | *194)* - Mickey Mouse Wall Watch | $25.00 | $30.00 |
| *145)* - Ceramic Pluto | $90.00 | $100.00 | *195)* - Gund's Big Bad Wolf Doll | $40.00 | $45.00 |
| *146)* - Ferdinand The Bull Wind-Up | $125.00 | $175.00 | *196)* - Pipsqueaks | $10.00 | $15.00 |
| *147)* - Snow White Tinkersand Pictures | $75.00 | $100.00 | *197)* - Christmas Plate By Schmid | $25.00 | $30.00 |
| *148)* - Snow White Wax Figurines | $100.00 | $115.00 | *198)* - Mickey Mouse Plastic Radio | $25.00 | $30.00 |
| **Modern Merchandise** | | | *199)* - Plastic Donald Duck Bath Toy | $15.00 | $20.00 |
| *149)* - Song Of The South Celluloid | $8,000.00 | $10,000.00 | *200)* - Mickey Mouse Candy Container | $125.00 | $175.00 |
| *150)* - Song Of The South Celluloid | $4,500.00 | $5,500.00 | *201)* - Mickey Mouse Bottle Warmer | $20.00 | $25.00 |
| *151)* - Disney Television Playhouse | $600.00 | $650.00 | *202)* - Item A - Mickey Mouse Megaphone | $3.00 | $5.00 |
| *152)* - Goebel's Bambi Ashtray | $175.00 | $200.00 | Item B - Donald Duck Ceramic Cup | $15.00 | $20.00 |
| *153)* - Mickey Mouse Belt Buckles | $75.00 | $100.00 | *203)* - Item A - Runner Tinkerbell | $5.00 | $7.00 |
| *154)* - Disney Character Store Display | $350.00 | $400.00 | Item B - Plastic Snow White | $5.00 | $7.00 |
| *155)* - Disneykin Display | $350.00 | $400.00 | Item C - Rubber Mickey Mouse | $5.00 | $10.00 |
| *156)* - Mickey Mouse Timex Watch | $150.00 | $200.00 | *204)* - Mickey Mouse Lamp | $20.00 | $25.00 |
| *157)* - Donald Duck Ceramic Figurine | $125.00 | $135.00 | *205)* - Disney Soakies | $20.00 | $25.00 |
| *158)* - Mickey Mouse Alarm Clock | $150.00 | $175.00 | *206)* - New Disneykins Play Set | $200.00 | $225.00 |
| *159)* - Mickey Mouse Disneykin Play Set | $100.00 | $125.00 | *207)* - Mickey Mouse Plastic Banks | $20.00 | $25.00 |
| *160)* - Mickey Mouse Weather House | $60.00 | $65.00 | *208)* - Mickey Mouse & Donald Duck | | |
| *161)* - Thumper and Flower Ceramics | $70.00 | $75.00 | Rubber Figures | $15.00 | $20.00 |
| *162)* - Mickey Mouse Watch | $175.00 | $195.00 | *209)* - Disney Puzzle Blocks | $5.00 | $10.00 |
| *163)* - Item A - Pooh Honey Bank | $25.00 | $30.00 | *210)* - Donald Duck Tin Tea Set | $50.00 | $75.00 |
| Item B - Pluto Cartoon Scissors | $10.00 | $15.00 | *211)* - Item A - Avon Mickey Container | $15.00 | $20.00 |
| *164)* - Dopey Clock | $45.00 | $50.00 | Item B - Rubber Minnie Mouse | $15.00 | $20.00 |
| *165)* - Donald The Bubble Duck | $50.00 | $55.00 | Item C - Plastic Minnie Mouse | $10.00 | $15.00 |
| *166)* - Donald Duck Jack In The Box | $250.00 | $275.00 | *212)* - Mickey Mouse Club Lunch Box | $50.00 | $75.00 |
| *167)* - Donald Duck Celluloid | $400.00 | $500.00 | *213)* - Bambi Ceramic Planter | $40.00 | $50.00 |
| *168)* - Disneykin Play Sets | $125.00 | $135.00 | *214)* - Item A - Mickey Mouse Watch | $50.00 | $60.00 |
| *169)* - Cinderella Watch | $100.00 | $110.00 | Item B - Mickey/Minnie Mouse Watch | $40.00 | $45.00 |
| *170)* - Cecil Munsey's "Disneyana" Book | $130.00 | $150.00 | Item C - Snow White U.S. | | |
| *171)* - Disneykin Television Scenes | $30.00 | $35.00 | Time Watch | $40.00 | $45.00 |
| *172)* - Disney Characters Figurine | $20.00 | $25.00 | Item D - Mickey Mouse Pocket Watch | $75.00 | $80.00 |
| *173)* - Disney Wall Plaques | $10.00 | $15.00 | *215)* - Item A - Donald Duck Tricky Toe | $30.00 | $35.00 |
| *174)* - Mickey Mouse Slugaroo | $20.00 | $25.00 | Item B - Goofy Ball Toy | $25.00 | $30.00 |
| *175)* - Babes In Toyland Soldier Set | $60.00 | $70.00 | *216)* - Mickey Mouse Pin | $300.00 | $325.00 |
| *176)* - Mickey & Minnie Mouse Silverware | $10.00 | $15.00 | *217)* - Mickey & Minnie Mouse Dolls | $10.00 | $15.00 |
| *177)* - Mickey And Minnie Mouse Puppets | $15.00 | $20.00 | *218)* - Mickey Mouse Rug | $40.00 | $45.00 |
| *178)* - Bambi Disneykin | $15.00 | $20.00 | *219)* - Mickey & Minnie Mouse Tea Set | $20.00 | $25.00 |
| *179)* - Ceramic Bambi Figurines | $150.00 | $175.00 | *220)* - Fire Fighters Lunch Box | $50.00 | $55.00 |
| *180)* - Donald Duck Pull Toy | $115.00 | $125.00 | *221)* - Item A - Mickey Mouse Gumball | | |
| *181)* - Casey Jr. Wall Design | $15.00 | $20.00 | Machine | $10.00 | $15.00 |
| *182)* - Item A - Mickey Mouse Doll | $10.00 | $15.00 | Item B - Mickey Mouse Plastic Bank | $20.00 | $25.00 |
| Item B - Tin Spinning Top | $5.00 | $10.00 | *222)* - Item A - Mickey Mouse Music Maker | $5.00 | $10.00 |
| Item C - Disneyland Button | $5.00 | $10.00 | Item B - Mickey Mouse Moving Toy | $5.00 | $10.00 |
| *183)* - Robert Lesser's "Celebration Of Comic | | | *223)* - Item A - Mickey Mouse Nodder | $35.00 | $40.00 |
| Art & Memorabilia" Book | $60.00 | $65.00 | Item B - Mickey Mouse Ball | $15.00 | $20.00 |
| *184)* - Pluto Ceramic Bank | $40.00 | $45.00 | *224)* - Mickey Mouse Candy Tin | $1.00 | $5.00 |
| *185)* - Rolykins | $35.00 | $40.00 | *225)* - Mickey Mouse Hard Rubber Figure | $5.00 | $10.00 |
| *186)* - Mushroom Ceramic Bowl | $300.00 | $325.00 | *226)* - Item A - Mickey Mouse Flashlight | $2.00 | $5.00 |
| *187)* - Item A - Mickey Tin Mousekabank | $5.00 | $10.00 | Item B - Mickey Mouse Little Treasure | $2.00 | $5.00 |
| Item B - Mickey Mouse Pez Dispenser | $1.00 | $5.00 | *227)* - Mickey's Musical Money Box | $10.00 | $15.00 |
| Item C - Mickey Mouse Card Game | $5.00 | $10.00 | *228)* - Mickey Mouse Plates | $5.00 | $10.00 |

# Schroeder's ANTIQUES Price Guide

. . . is the #1 best-selling antiques & collectibles value guide on the market today, and here's why . . .

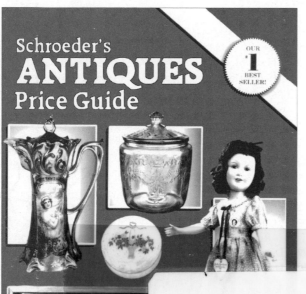

Schroeder's ANTIQUES Price Guide

OUR #1 BEST SELLER!

Identification & Values Of Ove...

8½ x 11, 608...

• *More than 300 advisors, well-known dealers, and top-notch collectors work together with our editors to bring you accurate information regarding pricing and identification.*

• *More than 45,000 items in almost 500 categories are listed along with hundreds of sharp original photos that illustrate not only the rare and unusual, but the common, popular collectibles as well.*

• *Each large close-up shot shows ... clearly. Every subject is ... tories and background ... e not found in any of ...ations.*

• *... ep abreast of newly ... n adding several new ... e need arises.*

If it merits the ... roeder's. And you can feel confident that ... ccurate. Our advisors thoroughly check ... ngs that may not be entirely reflective ... f merit. Only the best of the lot remains ...

Without doubt, you'll find
**SCHROEDER'S ANTIQUES PRICE GUIDE**
the only one to buy for
reliable information and values.

## cb
**COLLECTOR BOOKS**
*A Division of Schroeder Publishing Co., Inc.*